AQA English Language and Literature B

Unit 1: Introduction to language and literature study

Exclusively endorsed by AQA

AS

Christine Bennett
Chris Purple
Series editor
Chris Purple

Nelson Thornes

Published in 2011 by:
Nelson Thornes Ltd
Delta Place
27 Bath Road
CHELTENHAM
GL53 7TH
United Kingdom

11 12 13 14 15 / 10 9 8 7 6 5 4 3 2 1

A catalogue record for this book is available from the British Library

ISBN 978 1 4085 1556 3

Cover photograph Rachel Frank/Corbis

Page make-up by Pantek Media, Maidstone

Printed in Croatia by Zrinski

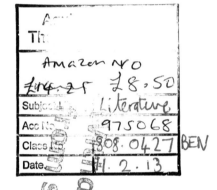

Acknowledgements

The author and the publisher would also like to thank the following for permission to reproduce material:

Px image from iStockphoto; p4 'Food Glorious Food' from *Oliver!* composed by Lionel Bart © 1959 by Lakeview Music Publishing Company Ltd. All rights reserved; p6 reproduced by permission of Oxford University Press from *Oxford Advanced Learners Dictionary 8th Edition* by A.S. Hornby © Oxford University Press 2010; p6 *Collins English Dictionary 10th Edition 2010* © William Collins Sons & Co. Ltd 2010 © HarperCollins Publishers 1991, 1994, 1998, 2010; p6 'food'. Roget's 21st Century Thesaurus, Third Edition. Philip Lief Group 2009 <thesaurus.com http://thesaurus.com/browse/food>; p8 © Witney Lakes Restaurant; p66 © Simpsons Fish and Chips, Cheltenham; p67 from *Cod: A Biography of the Fish That Changed the World* by Mark Kurlansky, published by Vintage Books. Reprinted by permission of The Random House Group Ltd; p68 from *Ghost Train to the Eastern Star* by Paul Theroux © Paul Theroux, 2008. All rights reserved; p68 from *Orchards in the Oasis* by Josceline Dimbleby, published by Quadrille Books. Reprinted by permission of the author; p69 Extracts from *The Oxford Children's Book of Science* by Charles Taylor and Stephen Pople (OUP, 1994) © Charles Taylor and Stephen Pople 1994, reprinted by permission of Oxford University Press; p70 From *The Year 1000* by Robert Lacey and Danny Danziger, published Little, Brown Book Group 1999. Reprinted by permission of Little, Brown Book Group; p70 webpage extract © Robert Genn.

Every effort has been made to contact copyright holders and we apologise if any have been overlooked. Should copyright have been unwittingly infringed in this publication the owners should contact the publishers, who will make the correction at reprint.

Contents

Introduction to this book

Nelson Thornes and AQA

Nelson Thornes has worked in collaboration with AQA to ensure that this book offers you the best support for your AS or A Level course and helps you to prepare for your exams. The partnership means that you can be confident that the range of learning, teaching and assessment practice materials has been checked by the senior examining team at AQA before formal approval, and is closely matched to the requirements of your specification.

How to use this book

This book covers the specification for your course and is arranged in a sequence approved by AQA. The introduction to the book explains what will be required of you as an English Language and Literature student. The book is divided into two units and each unit into two sections. Each section will prepare you for a certain type of question in your examination.

Unit 1 Section A introduces you to the study of language and literature by taking you through many of the texts in the AQA English Language and Literature B *Anthology for Unit 1: Food Glorious Food*. Unit 1 Section B gives detailed guidance on responding to questions on the Anthology texts and practical advice on preparing for the unseen text question. Unit 2 focuses on the coursework assignment. Unit 2 Section A explores thematic links and stylistic differences between the paired set texts, focusing on preparing you for writing your analytical coursework piece (Part A). Unit 2 Section B provides additional guidance on your creative writing piece (Part B).

Definitions of all key terms and any words that appear in bold can be found in the glossary at the back of this book.

The features in this book include:

Learning objectives

At the beginning of each unit you will find a list of learning objectives that contain targets linked to the requirements of the specification.

Key terms

Terms that you will need to be able to define and understand. These terms are coloured blue in the textbook and their definitions also appear in the glossary at the end of this book.

Research point

Suggestions for further research to enhance your studies and develop the kind of thinking that will help you achieve the highest grades in your English Language and Literature B course.

Links

Links to other areas in the textbook, or in your experience from GCSE, which are relevant to what you are reading.

Further reading

Links to further sources of information, including websites and other publications.

Think about it

Short activities that encourage reflection.

Background information

In Unit 1, information that will inform your study of a particular Anthology text.

Practical activity

Activities to develop skills, knowledge and understanding that will prepare you for assessment in English Language and Literature B.

Critical response activity

Activities that focus on a specific extract to develop skills relevant to your assessment in the examination.

AQA Examiner's tip

Hints from AQA examiners to help you with your study and to prepare you for your exam and coursework.

Commentary

Examples of answers you might give to the activities. These are designed to help you to understand what type of response the examiner is looking for, not to tell you the answer. There are many equally valid responses, so you will find this book most helpful if you try the activity yourself first and then look at the commentary to read another opinion. Not all activities have a commentary.

AQA examination questions are reproduced by permission of the Assessment and Qualifications Alliance.

Web links for this book

Because Nelson Thornes is not responsible for third-party content online, there may be some changes to this material that are beyond our control. In order for us to ensure that the links referred to are as up-to-date and stable as possible, please let us know at **webadmin@nelsonthornes.com** if you find a link that doesn't work and we will do our best to redirect these, or to list an alternative site.

Introduction to English Language and Literature

Integrated study of language and literature

The books in this series are designed to support you in your AS and A2 English Language and Literature studies. What is special about this subject is that it brings together aspects of two other kinds of A Level English course – the separate English Literature and English Language specifications – and there are real advantages in continuing your studies of English Language and Literature in an integrated course of this sort.

English at every level up to GCSE requires both language and literature to be studied as essential parts of the course. How can you study literature properly without being keenly interested in the medium of that literature – the ways in which words, sentences, paragraphs and chapters interrelate to create texts of various kinds? These texts may be novels, short stories, plays, documentary scripts, poems and non-fiction texts of a whole range of types and forms.

Being inquisitive about language in all of its forms and habitats is probably the most important quality that you can bring to your studies. We are immersed in language – it is our medium of communication with other people, it is the medium of entertainment (radio, television, comedy clubs, etc.) and a medium of instruction and information (how to … books, labels on medicines). More than that, my language and your language form essential parts of our identities, our individual personalities.

If you go on to study English at university, you will also encounter a subject which has largely abandoned sharp distinctions between 'literature' and 'language' study as unhelpful oversimplifications. You will inevitably be looking at how writers use language when you study a work of literature, and your knowledge about language and how it is used can help you to appreciate and understand how writers and speakers, readers and listeners can be creative and responsive in their experiences of language.

It is important not to think of A Level English Language and Literature as a mix-and-match course in which you 'do language' in one section of a unit and 'do literature' in another section. The point is that language study and literature study are integrated and you need to think about how your interest in language can extend and enhance your appreciation of literary texts. You also need to think about literary texts as examples of language being used in ways that repay close scrutiny, analysis and reflection. There are four main skills you need to develop during your AS and A2 course:

- You need to show that you are capable of reading texts closely and thoughtfully and writing about those texts in ways that show intelligent engagement and control.
- You need to show that you understand the characteristics of various kinds of spoken language, ranging from spontaneous exchanges between friends or strangers to carefully prepared speeches that are designed to persuade large numbers of people in live events or via television and radio.
- You need to show that you are capable of producing writing that is appropriate to the purpose and audience specified in the task, showing conscious control of your choices of vocabulary, grammar and structure.

You need to show that you are capable of writing in a focused and analytical way about your own writing – the processes you apply, the choices you make and the evaluation of whether the text works as well as you intended.

All of these activities build directly on the skills you have developed during your GCSE course and in your earlier secondary years, as well as in your primary school and during the pre-school years when you learned language skills by imitating adults and children with whom you grew up. These are skills that many of us continue to develop as the range of our experiences as readers, writers, speakers and listeners expands.

The units

This course focuses on a number of literary texts and on particular language topics. Here is a preview of each of the four units that make up the AS and A2 course.

Unit 1 (ELLB1): Introduction to language and literature study
Examination: 1 hour and 45 minutes

For this unit you will study an Anthology of thematically linked spoken and written texts. The Anthology covers the three main literary genres of prose fiction, poetry and drama as well as a range of non-literary texts. The theme for this Anthology (covering examinations in 2012, 2013 and 2014 only) is 'Food Glorious Food'. You will answer two questions, the first on an unseen text (or texts) which is thematically linked to the Anthology. The second question is set on the texts studied in the Anthology and will require you to comment on writers/speakers' uses of language and their attitudes towards a specified theme. This is an **open book examination**.

Unit 2 (ELLB2): Themes in language and literature
Coursework

The aim of this unit is to develop your reading and writing skills through the study of one pair of texts, selected from the six pairs available. Assessment is by a two-part coursework:

– Part A requires you to apply principles of literary and linguistic study to your chosen texts in order to explore the theme specified annually by AQA for each pair of texts (1,200 to 1,500 words).

– Part B requires you to demonstrate your understanding of one or both of your chosen texts by producing a piece of creative writing which extends and enhances the thematic discussion you completed in Part A (500 to 800 words).

Units 1 and 2 comprise the first year or AS part of the course:

Unit 3 (ELLB3): Talk in life and literature
Examination: 2 hours

The emphasis in this unit is on the ways meanings are constructed and conveyed in spoken language. You are required to study one play from a choice of four set plays, which will include at least one by Shakespeare. You will also be required to apply your literary and linguistic understanding to the study of a variety of transcripts of real-life spoken situations. This is a **closed book examination**.

Unit 4 (ELLB4): Text transformation
Coursework

This unit requires you to choose two literary works from a selection of prescribed authors and use them as the basis for the creation of a new

Think about it
Think about how much of your ability in the subject we call English is derived from your experiences in school and how much is derived from ordinary everyday contacts within your network of friends and family.

For example, if you focus on spoken language for the moment, have you considered how you acquired your accent? Have you ever consciously modified the way you speak or been told to by someone else? If so, what does this suggest about the range of attitudes to spoken language?

Key terms
Open book examination: an examination in which you are allowed to take unmarked copies of the books you have studied into the examination room and refer to them if you wish as you write your answers.

Closed book examination: an examination in which you are not allowed to take copies of the books you have studied into the examination room.

text or texts. The new text or texts must be of a different genre from the original and must be between 1,500 and 2,500 words. You also need to write a commentary or commentaries (1,000 to 2,000 words) in which you reflect on the transformation task in order to demonstrate understanding of the creative process.

Units 3 and 4 comprise the second year of the A Level course.

Preparation

How should you prepare for approaching your studies in this way? The essential points are that you need to:

- approach your reading and writing in an integrated way, building on both linguistic and literary understanding and methods
- develop your creativity and independence as you encounter both spoken and written language
- think about texts and the relationships between texts, which also requires that you think about the social, cultural and historical contexts of these texts
- develop independent ways of working so that your individual skills as a producer of spoken and written language are extended, and you also become increasingly thoughtful and responsive in your judgements and evaluations of the language you encounter as reader and as listener.

Assessment Objectives

You also need to be clear about the Assessment Objectives (AOs) that underpin all of your studies within this subject. Although the term Assessment Objective may sound a little remote and forbidding, you do need to understand their importance in order to study effectively and give yourself the best possible chance of achieving high grades.

Table 1 *Assessment Objectives for Unit 1*

Assessment Objectives	Questions to ask yourself
AO1 Select and apply relevant concepts and approaches from integrated linguistic and literary study, using appropriate terminology and accurate, coherent written expression	Can I write accurately and coherently about a range of texts of various sorts, using specialist linguistic and literary terms and concepts that will help me to be clear and precise?
AO2 Demonstrate detailed critical understanding in analysing the ways in which structure, form and language shape meanings in a range of spoken and written texts	Can I discuss and write about structure, form and language of spoken and written texts in ways that reveal my critical and analytical understanding?
AO3 Use integrated approaches to explore relationships between texts, analysing the significance of contextual factors in their production and reception	Can I use my linguistic and literary understanding to interpret and evaluate texts and to compare different texts and their social, cultural and historical contexts?

You will have noticed that running through the questions in Table 1 is an insistence on the need to apply your knowledge and understanding of both language and literature, and this is the key to success on this course of study.

■ How to read

In 2007 John Sutherland, a professor of English, published *How to Read a Novel*, subtitled 'A User's Guide'. This book, which is accessible and well worth reading, raises many issues relevant to your studies at AS and A2 Level in its 28 short chapters. Sutherland shows us the importance of developing autonomy as a reader – that is, approaching our reading thoughtfully and evaluating what we encounter for ourselves, and not uncritically accepting the opinions of others. In his final chapter, for example, Sutherland explains why, for him, Thackeray's *Vanity Fair* is one of the greatest English novels. He also quotes the philosopher Alain de Botton, who describes the book as 'the most overrated ever'. There could hardly be a sharper contrast between their opinions, yet each man is capable of developing a cogent and persuasive case in support of his judgement. You as a reader need to work towards developing your critical and thinking skills so that you can form judgements, advance them and defend them in discussion and writing. It is also important to take your time and hold back from making judgements about texts that you might find unusual or difficult to get to grips with. As far as your examination texts are concerned, you need to persevere especially with works that you find difficult on a first reading, and you need to be receptive to a range of critical and explanatory comment from your teachers, books or web sources. If you eventually judge a book to be flawed in some way and you can establish a clearly argued and well supported case, you will be demonstrating exactly the kinds of skills and understanding that will entitle you to high marks in the examinations or in your coursework. Look again at AO3 and the corresponding third question in Table 1.

Before you begin to think in detail about how to read a novel (or a play, poem or non-fiction text), you need to ask an even more fundamental question: Why am I reading this book? More specifically, what exactly is my purpose as a reader? At different times in your reading lives you will doubtless have a wide range of justifications or reasons for reading. Because you are following a course in English Language and Literature, it is a safe bet that you enjoy reading as a leisure activity and you value the contacts you have via the printed page with the thoughts, ideas, stories and experiences of others.

Of the myriad possible answers to the question 'Why am I reading this book?', perhaps the most likely is that you derive some kind of pleasure or satisfaction from doing so. However, for the reading you do as part of the English Language and Literature course, you will almost certainly have an additional reason, a pragmatic or utilitarian one; to achieve the highest possible grades as a passport to a university place or a career.

Different kinds of reading can fit into three main categories:

- ■ *Reading the lines:* reading for surface meanings. Much of our day-to-day reading takes place at this level: skimming a newspaper for details of what is on television, checking how long the ready meal needs in the microwave or reading a gossip column in a magazine, for example.
- ■ *Reading between the lines:* this requires the reader to be alert to what a text hints at or implies, as well as what is stated explicitly. This is the kind of careful 'reading in low gear' that you must engage in as you study your examination texts; they have been selected for study because they offer richness and complexity of various sorts. They are

■ Think about it

Think about the different types of reading in relation to the following quotations about how we read and what the effects of reading can be.

'Some books are to be tasted, others to be swallowed, and some few are to be chewed and digested.'
Francis Bacon (1561–1626)

'A conventional good read is usually a bad read, a relaxing bath in what we know already. A true good read is surely an act of innovative creation in which we, the readers, become conspirators.'
Malcolm Bradbury (1932–2000)

'Reading a book is like re-writing it for yourself ... You bring to a novel, anything you read, all your experience of the world. You bring your history and you read it in your own terms.'
Angela Carter (1940–92)

'There is creative reading as well as creative writing.'
Ralph Waldo Emerson (1803–82)

'Books give not wisdom where none was before. But where some is, there reading makes it more.'
John Harington (1561–1612)

'What is reading, but silent conversation.'
Walter Savage Landor (1775–1864)

not so much puzzles to be solved as creations of the writers' imaginations and they offer language and ideas which you, as a reader, need to interpret and enjoy on a number of levels, including the intellectual and the imaginative. You cannot study them adequately if you simply skim-read them and students who do not apply their skills of inference, evaluation and judgement will not be working in the ways necessary for success at AS, let alone A2, level.

■ *Reading beyond the lines:* this refers to the ability of readers to extend their thinking so that their understanding of a particular book is related to their experience of life, their knowledge of other books, their attitudes to moral issues, their judgements about artistic values – indeed, the whole of a reader's awareness of his or her world. Some books can affect us so much that we are forced to take stock of what we really believe and what we really feel; reading beyond the lines enables us to develop as individuals. We engage so closely with a book that we allow it to expand our awareness, our understanding, our values: it can help to make us, in some small way, different people after we have read the book from the people we were before.

■ Developing your skills

How can you best develop the skills and understanding necessary for success in your English Language and Literature B course? The obvious answer to that question is, of course, to study your set texts and language topics carefully, but that on its own is not enough. You also need to develop your ability to talk and write about books effectively, and that takes practice and a willingness to learn from others.

An excellent starting point is to listen to or watch radio or television programmes about books and reading. Here are some suggestions of programmes that will widen your knowledge:

■ *Bookclub* (Radio 4) brings a small panel of readers face to face with a writer to discuss one of his or her books. It is available on the BBC Radio website using the 'Listen Again' feature and gives an excellent insight into different readers' responses to the novel and the writer's approaches to writing.

■ *A Good Read* (Radio 4) involves discussion between three readers of a chosen book. Sometimes they agree about the merits of a particular book, but often they disagree. Listening to a discussion in which three intelligent readers express different views about the same book conveys a powerful message: what matters most is your personal response to books and your ability to explain and, where necessary, defend your position.

- *World Book Club* and *The Word* on the BBC Radio World Service – programmes can be listened to again via the website.
- *Emagazine* is a subscription magazine and website aimed specifically at all English A Level students with articles on a wide variety of authors and topics.
- Try reading book reviews in the Saturday editions of newspapers such as the *Guardian*, the *Independent*, the *Times* and the *Daily Telegraph* and their Sunday editions. These reviews will help to familiarise you with the process of evaluating and conveying to others your judgements and responses to your reading.

Remember, though, that the AS and A2 course is designed to develop your personal responses, and not to turn you into an obedient mouthpiece for the views of this critic or that critic. If you enter the examination room having acquired detailed knowledge of your set texts and topics, as well as independent judgement, you are well prepared for success in the exam, and the benefits that come from a lifetime's experience of being a good reader and a thoughtful writer.

This unit covers:

- learning about some of the important concepts and approaches that are relevant to AS Level English Language and Literature

- applying those concepts and approaches to the study of the texts in AQA's *Food Glorious Food* Anthology

- gaining an understanding of literary and linguistic terms and using those terms to help you talk and write about texts effectively

- developing your understanding of the characteristics of a wide range of literary and non-literary forms

- developing your ability to find points of similarity and difference between texts

- learning how to write about two texts that are linked thematically but may be different in form, purpose, genre, and historical and social context.

Introduction

This introductory chapter gives you an overview of what you need to do to achieve success in your Unit 1 examination. The unit is based on the study of AQA's Anthology, *Food Glorious Food*, a collection of 33 texts covering a wide range of forms and purposes, including poetry, drama, transcripts of spontaneous speech, journalism, advertising and other non-fiction forms.

To help you to study the Anthology, you will need to learn how to analyse texts. This will involve understanding how writers and speakers construct meaning by using language in particular ways. This unit will help you to understand specific terms that will assist you to write effectively about the texts. The glossary on pages 81–83 provides a useful list of such terms, but it is also worth keeping and adding to your own list in the file or notebook that you use throughout the course. There are also particular concepts and techniques that you need to understand in order to compare texts effectively.

Assessment

You will be assessed on this unit in an examination that lasts 1 hour and 45 minutes and consists of two questions:

- Question 1 requires you to write about two unseen texts, that is, texts you have not studied previously. These texts will be on the theme of 'food glorious food' and they will have been selected because they provide good opportunities for you to demonstrate the skills, techniques and understanding that you have acquired while studying the texts in the Anthology.

- Question 2 is based on the texts that you have studied in the Anthology. You will be given a specific focus in the question and then you need to select two suitable texts from the Anthology. You must write about these texts according to the particular focus set out in the question, so it is vital that your chosen texts are relevant to the task.

It is essential that in both questions you *compare* the texts you are dealing with. Comparing means identifying and commenting on the ways in which the texts display similarities and differences. It is not enough to deal with one text and then to deal with the second text. The most successful answers maintain a comparison of the two texts throughout and in the Unit 1 section of this book we will show you ways to do just that.

Question 1 is worth one-third (32) of the marks for this examination paper and Question 2 is worth two-thirds (64) of the marks. The texts that you encounter for Question 1 are unseen, so you will need time to read them closely and carefully before you begin to write your answer. This means that you will probably need to spend more than one-third of the time on Question 1 (about 40 minutes), which will leave you about 65 minutes for Question 2.

Some students prefer to answer Question 2 first. That can be a sensible strategy because you will be dealing with texts that you already know well and that can help to build your confidence before tackling the unseen texts.

The Assessment Objectives

The examiners who mark your scripts will assess your answers by considering how effectively you fulfil criteria contained within the three Assessment Objectives (AOs) that apply to Unit 1:

AO1 tests your ability to select and apply relevant concepts and approaches from integrated linguistic and literary study.	This means that you will need to understand how best to approach the study of each Anthology text, selecting from a range of possible approaches.
AO2 tests your ability to demonstrate detailed critical understanding in analysing the ways in which structure, form and language shape meanings in a range of spoken and written texts.	This means that you will need to analyse language, commenting on how choices of words and phrases, as well as the use of particular kinds of sentence patterns, influence the effects that writers and speakers have on readers and listeners.
AO3 tests your ability to use integrated approaches to explore relationships between texts, analysing and evaluating the significance of contextual factors in their production and reception.	This means that you will need to compare different texts, showing how they might be similar and how they might be different in the ways they convey meaning and influence the attitudes, feelings and actions of readers and listeners. The second part of AO3 focuses on 'contextual factors', which means that you will be expected to comment on the circumstances in which texts are spoken or written and heard or read.

Notice that all three AOs refer to *applied* knowledge and understanding. In other words, although you need to know about linguistic and literary terms, concepts and approaches, the real test is how you *use* your knowledge, understanding and skills to analyse texts and comment effectively on the differences and similarities between them.

Achieving success

So, what do you need to do to achieve your best possible result in your Unit 1 examination? You need to:

- gain a thorough knowledge and understanding of the texts in the *Food Glorious Food Anthology*
- develop a good knowledge and understanding of the key terms and concepts that you will encounter in later chapters of this book
- be able to structure your answers in ways that enable you to compare the texts you are writing about
- consider, in advance, the various ways in which the texts in the Anthology can be linked
- write two answers within the strict discipline of an examination of 1 hour and 45 minutes.

Also, remember that you need to apply your knowledge in situations that are not completely predictable. Question 1 presents you with unseen texts that you are unlikely to have read before. For Question 2 you will only know what the specific focus of the question is when you have opened the paper, and it is then up to you to decide which texts you are going to write about in response to that question.

Practical activity

Look at the table of contents (page 3) in the AQA Anthology. How many ways can you think of to group the 33 texts? At this stage do not read the texts themselves but place them into groups solely on the basis of the information given on page 3. Here are a few ideas to help you get started:

- Form (e.g. prose or poetry).
- Source (book, newspaper, website, etc.).
- Gender of writer.
- Purpose of text.
- Intended audience.

In addition to these, try to think of at least **two** other ways in which the texts could be grouped.

1 The Anthology: introducing the theme of 'food glorious food'

This chapter covers:

- exploring the title of the Anthology *Food Glorious Food*

- analysing the way in which the words of lyrics from *Oliver!* are structured

- introducing some key terms and concepts about patterns of word usage

- exploring some of the ways in which words and meanings can be studied within texts.

The title of the Anthology, *Food Glorious Food*, is taken from Lionel Bart's song of the same name in the musical *Oliver!*. Oliver and the other boys in the workhouse sing the song while they are waiting for their meagre daily serving of gruel, a thin, unappetising porridge made by boiling oatmeal in water.

■ Patterns and repetition

Read the lyrics of the song carefully and look out for the pattern of repetition of particular words and phrases. The phrase 'food glorious food' occurs six times in the 69 lines of the song, and the word 'food' occurs a total of 27 times. What is more interesting, however, is the pattern of usage of the word 'food'. If you can print out the lyrics, use a highlighter to track the occurrences of the word. The table (opposite page) shows the **collocations** of 'food' and a group of adjectives used in the song as **premodifiers**.

These adjectives all express extremely positive evaluations of food, as you might expect from workhouse boys for whom the daily diet is a thin gruel. The song represents a celebration of what they can only fantasise about. We also find 'Once again, food' and 'Oh food'. This last reference echoes the language of prayer (O Lord …), and both underline the intensity of the boys' desire for some relief from 'the same old gru…el!'

Food Glorious Food
[BOYS]
Is it worth the waiting for?
If we live 'til eighty four
All we ever get is gru…el!
Ev'ry day we say our prayer –
Will they change the bill of fare?
Still we get the same old gru…el!
There's not a crust, not a crumb
   can we find,
Can we beg, can we borrow, or
   cadge,
But there's nothing to stop us
   from getting a thrill
When we all close our eyes and
   imag…ine

Food, glorious food!
Hot sausage and mustard!
While we're in the mood –
Cold jelly and custard!
Pease pudding and saveloy!
What next is the question?
Rich gentlemen have it, boys –
In-di-gestion!

Food, glorious food!
We're anxious to try it.

Three banquets a day –
Our favourite diet!
Just picture a great big steak –
Fried, roasted or stewed.
Oh, food,
Wonderful food,
Marvellous food,
Glorious food.

Food, glorious food!
What is there more handsome?
Gulped, swallowed or chewed –
Still worth a king's ransom.
What is it we dream about?
What brings on a sigh?
Piled peaches and cream, about
Six feet high!

Food, glorious food!
Eat right through the menu.
Just loosen your belt
Two inches and then you
Work up a new appetite.
In this interlude –
The food,
Once again, food
Fabulous food,
Glorious food.

Food, glorious food!
Don't care what it looks like –
Burned!
Underdone!
Crude!
Don't care what the cook's like.
Just thinking of growing fat –
Our senses go reeling
One moment of knowing that
Full-up feeling!

Food, glorious food!
What wouldn't we give for
That extra bit more –
That's all that we live for
Why should we be fated to
Do nothing but brood
On food,
Magical food,
Wonderful food,
Marvellous food,
Fabulous food,

[OLIVER]
Beautiful food,
[BOYS]
Glorious food.

■ The Anthology

The Anthology is not intended to be merely a celebration of food. Between them, the 33 texts have a great range and diversity and are unified only in the sense that their subject is food. In their various ways the Anthology texts target different audiences and serve many different purposes, including those that you may recall from your GCSE English course that describe various types of writing:

- inform
- explain
- describe
- analyse
- review
- comment
- argue
- persuade
- advise.

Some of the 33 texts fit more than one of these categories while others do not fit any of them comfortably.

Each one of the texts offers plenty of 'food for thought', which is a phrase that one dictionary defines as 'something that warrants serious consideration'. As we shall see in the analysis of crisp packets in Chapter 2, even the briefest text has linguistic features and meanings that will be illuminated if you apply the skills of close analysis. These are the skills that you will learn to develop during your English Language and Literature course.

Noun phrases		
Premodifiers (adjectives)	Headword (noun)	Frequency
Glorious		9
Wonderful		2
Marvellous	Food	2
Fabulous		2
Magical		1
Beautiful		1

■ Key terms

Collocation: the tendency of writers and speakers to place particular words in proximity with each other, such as 'Happy Father's Day' or 'Merry Christmas' (but not 'Merry Father's Day'). Collocations are often highly context dependent.

Premodifier: in a noun phrase such as 'a nasty knock on the nose', the premodifier is the word or phrase that precedes the noun 'knock'. Post-modifiers occur after the phrase. So 'nasty' is a premodifier that tells us more about the noun, and 'on the nose' is a post-modifier that gives us additional information.

■ Critical response activity

1 How many specific foods are mentioned in the song 'Food Glorious Food'? What are they, and how 'glorious' do they seem to you?

2 What do the premodifying adjectives in the table have in common? In what other contexts might you expect these words to be used?

3 What other aspects of the language of the song stand out as interesting? Look at the structure of the song and see how many different types of patterning of the language you can find.

■ Practical activity

The following quotations are all about food and eating. Consider each one and jot down what point or points you think the writer intended to make. Do you think their meanings are limited to food itself (literal meanings), or do some of them have more extended, or figurative, meanings?

Quotation	Source
'Tell me what you eat, and I will tell you what you are.'	Anthelme Brilla-Savarin (1755–1826)
'Nothing would be more tiresome than eating and drinking if God had not made them a pleasure as well as a necessity.'	Voltaire (1694–1778)
'Don't dig your grave with your own knife and fork.'	English proverb
'To eat is a necessity, but to eat intelligently is an art.'	La Rochefoucauld (1613–80)
'Those who think they have no time for healthy eating, will sooner or later have to find time for illness.'	Edward Stanley (1826–93)
'With eager feeding, food doth choke the feeder.'	Shakespeare (1564–1616)
'Bad men live that they may eat and drink, whereas good men eat and drink that they may live.'	Socrates (469 BCE–399 BCE)

And, finally here are two definitions from *The Devil's Dictionary* by Ambrose Bierce (1842–1913):

Edible: good to eat and wholesome to digest, as a worm to a toad, a toad to a snake, a snake to a pig, a pig to a man, and a man to a worm.

Eat: to perform successively (and successfully) the functions of mastication, humectation, and deglutition.

(You might need to look up some of the words in a dictionary, but think about what they mean before you do so.)

■ Exploring the meaning of words

The word 'food' is used so frequently that we seldom pause to think about it as a word. We all know what food is, but how does a dictionary define the word? The 2010 edition of the *Oxford Advanced Learner's Dictionary of Current English* (intended for students learning English) defines food as:

things that people or animals eat

The single-volume 2010 edition of the *Collins English Dictionary* gives these more detailed definitions:

1. any substance containing nutrients, such as carbohydrates, proteins and fats, that can be ingested by a living organism and metabolized into energy and body tissue
2. nourishment in more or less solid form as opposed to liquid form: food and drink
3. anything that provides mental nourishment or stimulus food for thought.

Reproduced from *Collins English Dictionary* © 2010 HarperCollins Publisher Ltd

■ Etymology of words

It is interesting to find out something about the history of the word 'food'. Some dictionaries also include information about the **etymology** of words. The *Chambers Dictionary of Etymology* (1988) lists various forms such as *fode, foode, foda* and *fodor* dating from about 1000. This dictionary also shows links between the English word and similar words in other European languages.

Here is the entry for food from an online thesaurus:

Main Entry: food

Part of Speech: noun

Definition: edible material

Synonyms: aliment, bite*, board, bread, cheer, chow, comestible, cookery, cooking, cuisine, diet, drink, eatable, eats, entrée, fare, fast food, feed, fodder*, foodstuff, goodies, grit, groceries, grub, handout, home cooking, keep, larder, meal, meat, menu, mess*, moveable feast, nourishment, nutriment, nutrition, pabulum, provision, ration, refreshment, slop, snack, store, subsistence, support, sustenance, table, take out, tuck, viand, victual, vittles

Antonyms: beverage, drink

* = informal/non-formal usage

Roget's 21st Century Thesaurus, Third Edition © 2009 by the Philip Lief Group.
http://thesaurus.com/browse/food

You may not have encountered all of these words before, but they are all **synonyms** or partial synonyms for food. They have very different associations and in ordinary usage they are far from interchangeable terms. For example, some pubs serving food use the label 'pub grub', but it is unlikely that a restaurant would use such a downmarket term as 'grub'. Fine cuisine will offer you a menu rather than a grub list. One word of very restricted use which does not occur in the list is 'snap', which was a term used by miners, especially in the Midlands and the north of England, for the food they took with them on their shifts underground. There are probably many other dialect words, or words used in particular industries, that have not found their way into thesaurus entries for food.

■ Key terms

Etymology: the study of the origins and historical development of word meaning and usage.

Synonym: word that has the same or very similar meaning to another, such as bucket/pail.

■ Research point

For more information on the etymology of the word 'food' look at this website: www.enotes.com/food-encyclopedia/etymology-food.

■ Practical activity

Just for fun, try this online quiz based on the etymology of some food words: www.funtrivia.com/trivia-quiz/Humanities/Interesting-Origins-of-Food-Related-Words-191100.html.

Look at the two **antonyms** that are given in the thesaurus, 'beverage' and 'drink'. There are many other words for drink that could be added to the list, some of which have specific associations. What would be served as a 'wee dram', or a 'cuppa', or a 'tipple' or a 'bevy' or 'plonk'?

Key terms

Antonym: word that has the opposite meaning to another, such as alive/dead.

Practical activity

1 Consider each of the words in the list of synonyms in the thesaurus entry on page 6 and decide in which context they are each most likely to be used. Decide whether the word is:

  a in widespread use
  b used in a particular part of the country
  c used mainly by a particular age group
  d used more in formal situations
  e used more in informal situations
  f restricted in its usage in some other way.

2 Can you or your parents or grandparents suggest any other words for food that are missing from the thesaurus entry?

Research point

There are many online resources that can help you to understand the grammatical terms you need to learn and apply to the analysis of texts. This one is particularly helpful: www.englishbiz.co.uk/grammar/main_files/definitionsa-m.htm.

Many words for food and drink have a surprisingly long history. Apart from trade names, very few new food words have been introduced in the past 50 years – there is just one in the list below. Can you think of any others? The earliest dates are approximations derived from various sources, but the recent dates are more exact. The fact that the word 'coffee' was first recorded in about 1600 does not mean that it was in common usage then. The word and the product became much more familiar when instant coffee was invented and distributed to the mass market in the UK after the Second World War.

Food words	Earliest date	Food words	Earliest date	Food words	Earliest date
Wine	725	Asparagus	1395	Chutney	1810
Beer	725	Scone	1510	Lager	1855
Corn	750	Chocolate	1600	Sushi	1893
Pea	800	Coffee	1600	Hamburger	1908
Bread	950	Omelette	1610	Pizza	1935
Bean	1000	Soup	1650	Burger	1939
Herring	1130	Muffin	1700	Fish finger	1962
Barley (baerlic)	1180 (960)	Whiskey	1715	Muesli	1900
Pudding	1285	Crumpet	1770	Balti	1980
Pasty	1300	Naan	1780		

2 Exploring language, meaning and context

Key terms

Semantics: the study of the system of meanings within a language.

Ambiguity: the possibility of interpreting written or spoken words in more than one way. Sometimes words are used in an unintentionally ambiguous way, but creative or humorous language can use ambiguity deliberately to achieve particular effects.

Semantics

In this chapter we need to think about *meaning* or, to use the technical term from linguistics, **semantics**. The concept of meaning is not as straightforward as we might think. In ordinary conversations we sometimes need to ask the question: 'What do you mean by that?' It could be that the speakers do not convey meaning clearly. Perhaps they make wrong assumptions about how far we share the background knowledge that is relevant to what is being said. Occasionally we fail to express our intended meaning as effectively as we want to because we cannot think of the right words to convey exactly what we intend to say.

Practical activity

The following is part of a weekly email sent to customers by Ross Drummond, manager of The Restaurant @ Witney Lakes Resort:

> It is not always the ingredients that sell the dish; it can sometimes be just how the dish is worded that attracts people to it or not. On Thursday last week our pies (which let me say were pretty good) sold like hot … pies. Beef cheek and kidney sold really well off the board on Thursday and then on Friday I put it on the board at lunch as ox cheek and kidney and sold none … not even a nibble.

Can you think of any reasons why customers should have found beef cheek and kidney pie more appealing than the same dish presented as ox cheek and kidney pie?

Utterances that may be understood in more than one way are ambiguous, that is, the words have two or more different meanings and can be interpreted in different ways. Sometimes the **ambiguity** is intentional; sometimes it is not. Some jokes depend upon wordplay, creating humour from the fact that words often have more than one meaning. For example, 'The Association of Atheists is a non-prophet organisation' is ambiguous when you hear the words but not when you see them written down. Some headlines are also, by accident or design, ambiguous, as shown in the following examples. In each case the opening sentence of the story resolves the ambiguity.

EXAM REPLACED AFTER PAPERS LEAKED

Hundreds of A-level students have had to sit a replacement exam after it was discovered papers had been leaked.

Reading closes physics department

The University of Reading is to close its physics department, this month's intake of 30 students being the last.

Sometimes we play with meaning by deliberately saying the opposite of what we mean. If a friend is acting in a decidedly grumpy way, we might say: 'You're in a good mood this morning!' Our tone of voice and our facial expression will normally signal our sarcastic or comic intent, and we would not expect the friend to respond as if our words were meant to be taken at face value.

Connotative and denotative meanings

Before we go on to look at the ways in which meanings are created and used for particular effects in texts from the Anthology, we need to understand the important distinction between **connotative** and **denotative** meanings. Denotative meaning refers to the straightforward, literal meaning of a word as it might be applied to an animate or inanimate thing. Connotative meanings are the more individualised meanings that we might attach in ways that go beyond the literal meaning of a word.

Connotative meanings are, in a sense, individually created meanings that depend upon how our own personal attitudes are affected by particular words. *Spider.* To an arachnophobe, the sudden appearance of that word may arouse strong emotions of fear or disgust, whereas to a zoologist specialising in the study of arachnids a very different kind of response is likely. The two people bring different attitudes and expectations to the word, and they react differently according to their emotional and rational responses. The word carries sharply differing connotations even though there would be little disagreement about the denotative meaning of the word.

A denotative meaning of the word 'cat' is 'a small, domestic, fur-covered animal often kept as a pet'. Whichever dictionary we use, it will give a definition that covers this core meaning. The word 'cat' in itself tells us nothing about whether the speaker or writer likes cats or hates them. The word is neutral in terms of the attitudes of the user of the word. However, 'catty' does not mean 'like a cat'; it is a word that is seldom, if ever, applied to cats. Instead it describes a type of human behaviour. Is it equally likely to be applied to men *and* women, or is it more frequently applied to women's behaviour?

'Catty' carries strong connotative meanings. When the word is applied to a person it delivers an adverse judgement because a negative evaluation is inherent in the word itself.

■ Applying meaning to texts

Text 23: The Jonathan Crisp packet

When you are analysing texts (especially *multimedia texts*), it is important to consider the presentation and **juxtaposition** of the various features and pieces of text that make up the whole. Juxtaposition is the placing together (or in close proximity) of visual or textual elements specifically to draw out comparisons or contrasts. Graphics and design features are prominent elements of Text 23 and Text 24 (the second crisp packet), and it is important to think about the relationship between the linguistic and visual aspects in texts of this sort. **Graphology** is the term that refers to the study of writing systems, including the use of fonts of different styles and sizes. Graphics refers more widely to the overall design of the texts including photographs, diagrams and other visual elements.

Note that you will study texts in the Anthology that do not have any significant design features and so there will be no point in commenting about design in such texts. In the examination it is best to write about graphological features only when they are significant in the texts that you are comparing, and make sure that you focus on the precise wording of the question. Your main focus should always be on the language of the texts.

Graphological features are important aspects of Text 23. The front of the Jonathan Crisp packet (Text 23) contains relatively few words, but the feature that is immediately striking is the head-and-shoulders caricature of a sweaty, stern-looking man sporting an extravagant red moustache and bushy red eyebrows. The graphic design of the front of the packet is an integral part of this text and we need to try to analyse the intentions and purposes of the team, including the writers and graphic designers, who collaborated to design the crisp packet.

Critical response activity

1. In pairs or small groups look at Text 23 (the Jonathan Crisp packet) and make notes on your response to the following question: 'What purposes are served by the packaging of snack-food products such as crisps?'

   Below are some possible answers. Consider each one in relation to Text 23 and place them in rank order according to your judgement about their relative importance. Consider the front and back of the packet separately and if necessary devise different rank orders for the front of the packet and the back of the packet.

   a Create humour.
   b Carry information which must by law be provided for consumers.
   c Identify the flavour of the crisps.
   d Establish a clear product image.
   e Protect the contents.
   f Attract the attention of potential buyers.
   g Distinguish the brand from other rival brands.

   Are there any other points that you think should be added to the list?

2. Compare your rank orders with those of other students and discuss any differences that might exist.

3. Overall, how successful do you think the Jonathan Crisp design is?

Context of production

Any text exists within a particular situation and for a particular set of purposes, and this is called its **context of production**. The exact nature of where a text occurs and what it is intended to achieve exerts a powerful influence on the language choices made by the writer or speaker in conveying intended meanings and emphases. When we evaluate the success or effectiveness of any text it is important to relate it to the context in which it occurs.

Consider Texts 23 and 24 (the two crisp packets) in the Anthology. The context is highly specific: the packaging of a snack product which, as soon as the contents are eaten, will be discarded. Despite this, it is clear that the design and language are crafted very carefully. Our task in analysing these two texts is to ask the questions 'Why?' and 'What?':

- *Why* did the writers and designers make the many choices that resulted in these texts?
- *What* responses and reactions did the writers want to draw from their customers in response to these texts?

The following table shows you how to analyse the content of the front of the Jonathan Crisp packet. By looking closely at each aspect of the text and the design of the packet we can build up a good understanding of how the design and language try to influence readers who are also, of course, customers and consumers. Before looking at the table, consider the following questions:

- *Does the fact that the name Jonathan Crisp is presented in a handwritten italic style affect its connotative meaning or the likely response of potential buyers?*
- *What are the associations or connotations of both the name and the style of handwriting combined?*

Words from text	Commentary
JALAPENO PEPPER	A variety of chilli pepper producing a warm, spicy sensation when eaten. The mention of a particular variety of chilli pepper may contribute to the upmarket image. Would the more common 'chilli pepper' have had quite the same sense of class if that had been used as the name for the flavour of these crisps? Does 'Jalapeño' have more exotic connotations than 'chilli'?
Crisps of Natural Character	It is written in the same stylish handwriting as the signature 'Jonathan Crisp'. What are the connotations of the words 'natural' and 'character'? What image is being cultivated by the use of these words? Notice how the word 'character' appears in the closest proximity to the caricature of The Colonel.
A GLORIOUS 40g e SIZE	A combination of the legally required declaration of the weight of the product and the surprising word 'glorious'. What are the connotations of this word? Does it suggest that the packet is larger than those of rival brands, or does it suggest that the crisps themselves are superior in some way?
MADE HERE IN OLD BLIGHTY	Encircling a small silhouette map of England, Wales and Scotland, these words are used instead of the more usual 'Made in England' or 'Produced in the UK'. 'Blighty' was an affectionate term used for the home country (usually England) by British soldiers abroad during the First World War (1914–18). It has strong associations with 'good old home' and is far more emotive than the usual wording for the country of origin of a product. (Despite the cultivation of a strong sense of tradition and 'Englishness', the crisps are actually made on an industrial estate near Crumlin in South Wales.)

Register

Within these short pieces of text there are some unexpected deviations from the usual language of product packaging. The word that linguists use for a variety of language used for a particular purpose or within a particular social context is **register**. In Text 23 some of the normal expectations about register are flouted, and it is reasonable to suppose that this was a deliberate strategy intended to serve a purpose. The most striking example occurs in the third and fourth rows in the table above, but we shall also find others on the reverse side of the packet.

Now look at the reverse side of the Jonathan Crisp packet. There is considerably more written text, and it is concentrated in the right-hand column where information that is required by law is set out.

- Ingredients and allergy/dietary information.
- Nutritional information.
- Packet size and symbol showing responsible disposal of used packaging.
- Packet size and storage advice.
- Name and address of the company producing the product.
- Bar code.
- Guarantee.

All of these elements are conventionally written within the normal register for product information. The '40 g e' size does not have the word 'glorious' attached, as it did on the front of the packet, and there is no attempt to individualise the wording to distinguish it from that used on other brands of potato crisps. Notice that most of the information provided is not presented in continuous prose but in lists and tables.

Key terms

Register: variety of language that is used for particular purposes or within a particular social context.

Critical response activity

Look closely at Text 23 (the front of the crisp packet) and answer the following questions:

1 What purpose do you think is served by each element of the front-of-packet design?

   a   Text – language.

   b   Images.

   c   Graphology.

   What do you think is their combined effect?

2 Taking all of the words and images into account, whom do you think the marketing team regards as its target customers in terms of age, social class and gender?

The main exception to this is the wording of the guarantee, the final section on the reverse of the packet. (See Critical response activity.)

The language used in the left column of the Jonathan Crisp packet is a very different matter. It includes a personalised account of the inspiration for the development of this crisp flavour that reveals something of the identity of the cartoon character depicted on the front. He is 'The Colonel' and his opinion of the crisps is quoted:

'By Jove, they pack a jolly welcome punch, Jonathan.'

What do these words suggest about the character and background of The Colonel? Who uses the exclamation 'By Jove' nowadays and how widespread is the adverbial use of 'jolly' to premodify the adjective 'welcome'?

The section that follows shows Jonathan echoing some of The Colonel's language:

'Must say I was suitably chuffed'	**Ellipsis** in sentence structure, with omission of subject 'I'; dated language in lexical choice of 'chuffed'.
'spirited little fellows'	Quaint personification of the crisps to refer to their spicy flavour.
'spicy fodder'	Use of 'fodder', a word usually applied to animal feed, exemplifies The Colonel's distinctive choices of lexis. It is intended to be amusing – at least to the target audience for these crisps.
'foreign johnnies'	Dated and disrespectful way of referring to non-British people, again suggesting something of The Colonel's attitudes through his choice of lexis. For some people the Colonel's language would be offensive. Others might say that the phrase is harmlessly light-hearted. How risky do you think this kind of humour might be? Does it tell us something about the group of consumers Jonathan Crisp is targeting?
'hotter climes'	The *Collins English Dictionary* lists 'clime' as: 'Poetic. A region or its climate'. It is also sometimes used in a disparaging or mocking way, similar to the connotations of 'foreign johnnies' above.

Text 24: The Salty Dog crisp packet

Having looked at Text 23 in some detail we now turn to Text 24, the Salty Dog crisp packet.

If we compare the packet fronts, there are some similarities. Both use cartoon drawings, although the subjects differ as do the cartoon styles used to depict The Colonel and Salty Dog.

Because graphic design is an integral part of Texts 23 and 24, it is essential to consider their design features as part of the analysis. However, most of your analysis should focus on the language features and it is important not to devote too much time to graphology.

Critical response activity

In the same way that you analysed Text 23, examine Text 24 closely and make notes on the ways in which the crisp packet uses particular *images and language techniques* to create a *distinctive product image*.

The following prompts should guide you through your analysis:

■ graphology
■ text (use of different fonts and sizes)
■ use of humour
■ product information
■ jokes and audience involvement
■ nutritional information (note how the language used is 'the nutritional info' not the unabbreviated 'information' – what effect does this create?).

Commentary

Key words in the question are 'images and language techniques' and 'distinctive product image', so your notes should have assembled points that build up a link between these two aspects. The task is not simply to describe Text 24 but to select particular images and language techniques and show how they contribute to establishing a distinctive Salty Dog image for the product. Here are some points that would be relevant to the question:

■ **Graphic design**: the immediate impression is one of simple, almost amateurish design. The stylised drawing of Salty Dog is in the centre of the packet with the roughly printed and slightly askew words 'Salty' above and 'Dog' below. The impression given is not one of sophistication, and this is reinforced by the inconsistent printed lettering in which upper-case and lower-case letters are apparently randomly thrown together. On the reverse of the packet the distinctive lettering for the product name is repeated and there are two more images of an equally scruffy Salty Dog. The effect of this seems to be to suggest that Salty Dog is a plain, straightforward, no-nonsense brand.

■ **Text – fonts and sizes**: the key words are made prominent by their size (Salty Dog) and by white-on-black boxes (SEA salt & black PEPPER). Less prominent are the slogans 'THE hand-COOKED CRISPS … THAT bite BACK', which seem to suggest a distinctively strong flavour. This links with the simple and unsophisticated graphics that suggest Salty Dog crisps are plain and honest. Some people might find the 'errors' in the use of upper- and lower-case lettering are irritating, but such people are probably not seen by the company as their potential customers.

■ **Humour**: the company name Salty Dog is an unusual and amusing choice. The graphics themselves have an air of light-heartedness, with the endearingly scruffy dog that has eyes that do not quite match. The slogan presents the crisps as ones that 'bite back'. Together these elements position the company as different, individualistic and even quirky. The text at the foot of the packet front offers an amusing fiction about Salty Dog himself digging up 'the biggest & best potatoes'. Like him, they 'are a bit rough round the edges' and the joke about these being crisps that bite back is repeated. The company's

Practical activity

Food and confectionery packaging provides a rich and easily acquired source for textual comparison, with the bonus of being able to enjoy the contents later.

Compare the text and design of two or more other products within the same food category, such as Scotts and Quaker porridge oats, Kelloggs and supermarket own-brand corn flakes, and different brands of tea. Fair Trade tea and coffee packaging often provides an interesting contrast with non-Fair Trade market leaders.

address is given as 'Salty Towers', which is a humorous echo of the name of the TV comedy series *Fawlty Towers*. They are not, it seems, worried that the possible association with the shambolic business run by Basil Fawlty might tarnish their own image.

- **Product information**: the company describes itself as 'a small family business'. It tells us: 'We really care about the quality of our crisps', which conveys the sense that there is a personal commitment to high standards. The emphasis on the crisps being 'hand-cooked' also suggests that the production processes are not on an industrial scale and that there is a personal involvement in the production of the crisps.

- **Jokes and audience involvement**: the back of the packet contains a 'howler or growler?' section that prints a joke and invites Salty Dog customers to text in their own jokes, with some of the cost of texting going to support the Hearing Dogs for Deaf People charity. This presents the company as not merely enjoying humour, but using it in support of its own good cause, which appropriately relates to dogs. This could simply be an example of the company genuinely using its packaging as a medium for supporting a cause that it cares about, but there might also be some commercial benefit from being seen as a company with a social conscience.

- **Nutritional information**: the nutritional information on the back of the packet is required by law, but the company presents it in a slightly less formal way by using the abbreviation 'info', which helps to humanise its image. This is the section of the text that provides least opportunity for the company to create a distinctive product image.

Comparing Texts 23 and 24

Critical response activity

You should now be ready to attempt a comparative analysis of Texts 23 and 24 by answering the following question:

- Compare the ways in which Texts 23 and 24 try to achieve distinctive and memorable product images through their use of text and design features.

Remember to build in comparative comments and ensure that all of the comments you make are relevant to the precise wording of the question. Once you have completed your answer read the answer below. Compare the points you have made in your answer with those in the answer below.

Sample response

There are other points that the student who produced this answer could have made, but considering the limited time available, a detailed and effective response has been produced.

Each paragraph focuses on a particular aspect of the techniques used to 'achieve memorable and distinctive product images'.

Because Texts 23 and 24 are both taken from crisp packets it is not surprising that they share some common features. Each uses distinctive graphics to create an immediately recognisable and memorable product image. In the case of Jonathan Crisp, the most striking feature is the caricature image of a sweaty, elderly man with bushy red eyebrows and moustache, later revealed by the text as 'The Colonel'. The Salty Dog packet features a cartoon-style drawing of a small dog with the large lettering 'Salty' above and 'Dog' below the drawing. Even before we read the text on each packet in detail, the distinctive characters associated with each product are clearly displayed. For some consumers brand loyalty is important and the packaging of each product achieves immediate recognition. Both packets also depend on the visual humour of cartoon-style characters, one human and the other animal, to imply that the products are associated with fun and light-heartedness. This may enhance their customer appeal as impulse buys when they are displayed prominently in shops or pubs.

Each company also uses the written text and graphological design features to create distinctive product images. Lexical choices create brand images that reflect distinctive qualities. Jonathan Crisp presents its product as 'Crisps of Natural Character' and Salty Dog's product is 'The hand-cooked crisps that bite back'. Within each of these noun phrases is an evaluative adjective element – 'natural' and 'hand-cooked'. 'Natural' carries connotations of healthy goodness (as opposed to containing synthetic and unhealthy ingredients), and 'hand-cooked' suggests small-scale production processes in which skilled staff oversee the cooking.

The front of each packet displays prominently the name of the company producing the crisps, but the connotations are very different. The confident flourish of the handwritten signature 'Jonathan Crisp' serves both as company name and memorable design image, but by including the surname 'Crisp' it also creates a strong link between the generic product name and the company name, which is a clever promotional ploy. The Salty Dog packet is (apparently deliberately) less polished in its design and artwork. Although the packet is readily recognised as containing crisps, the name 'Salty Dog' is not immediately linked with the contents of the packet. The small font text needs to be read before the significance of the name becomes clear. There is a semantic link between the adjective 'salty' and the traditional inclusion of salt as a flavouring for crisps. The post-modification of 'crisps' by the phrase 'that bite back' reinforces the suggestion that these crisps are strongly flavoured, probably with a noticeable piquancy. It is notable too that the flavourings used are not merely 'salt' and 'pepper'; the salt is 'sea salt' and the pepper is 'black pepper', with the adjectives investing, or at least suggesting, special superior qualities to the crisps inside. In a similar way Jonathan Crisp uses not merely 'pepper' but 'Jalapeño pepper', and whether or not this has any effect on the flavour, it may carry connotations of superiority.

Although not immediately apparent at a first glance, both companies create a narrative around the crisps and the selection of product names. In the case of Jonathan Crisp this is conveyed by the short text in the first column of the reverse of the packet. The reported dialogue between The Colonel and Jonathan Crisp himself (both of whom are almost certainly invented characters) focuses on the delicious spicy flavour of the crisps and the authenticity of the flavour, measured against the Colonel's experiences of 'spicy fodder' in 'foreign climes'. The register of this paragraph is surprisingly uncharacteristic of food packaging; it takes the reader back to an earlier age by means of the speakers' dated lexis ('By Jove', 'suitably chuffed', 'spicy fodder cooked up by foreign johnnies'). This lexis is almost a caricature of the language of 19th century colonial civil servants, and in the next paragraph the reference to 'nanny' also takes us into a social context that is far removed from that of most people. The Salty Dog narrative is more mundane, describing the dog's activity of digging up 'only the biggest & best potatoes'. The text also contains amusing puns and other forms of wordplay ('Like Salty, our crisps are a bit rough round the edges' and 'howler or growler'), and the guarantee invites customers to contact the company if the product 'doesn't meet Salty's usual high standards'.

Although the product images created for Jonathan Crisp and Salty Dog differ markedly, each company succeeds in establishing a memorable image for its product. It would be interesting to set up an experiment to test consumers' responses to the two brands and to identify whether or not significant gender, class and age differences are apparent.

> Comparisons are built into each of the paragraphs in this sample response. The answer achieves a good balance between points of similarity and points of difference in the two texts.

> It is also clear that the candidate has secure knowledge of some key linguistic terms and is able to apply them so that relevant comments are made precisely and economically and are accompanied by textual evidence to support them. Above all, the answer shows that the candidate has read the two texts closely and analytically.

■ **Key terms**

Colloquial: informal language of the kind used in everyday speech.

Syntax: the way in which words are arranged to show the meaning. The word originates from the Greek word for arrangement: syntaxis.

Commentary

How analytical frameworks can be applied to Texts 23 and 24

Analytical framework	Explanation	Relevance to Texts 23 and 24
Phonology	Phonology is the term that refers to the study of the sound system of a language. The distinct units of sound are phonemes.	Because these are written texts with strong visual elements, it is not necessary to comment on phonology. However, in the Jonathan Crisp text the first column on the back of the packet uses dialogue and first person address to create a representation of the spoken styles of The Colonel and Jonathan. The lexical and stylistic choices in the written text suggest particular accents and voice qualities in these two characters.
Lexis (also referred to as lexical items, vocabulary and words)	Lexis is the linguistic term for the vocabulary used in a text. Lexical items belong to one of two classes: open and closed. Open class lexical items are nouns, verbs, adjectives and adverbs, and new words are added to the word stock of the four open class lexical categories. Closed class lexical items have a grammatical or structural function and include conjunctions, prepositions, pronouns and determiners. The term 'closed' is applied because it is extremely rare for new words having these grammatical functions to enter the language.	The lexical range found in Texts 23 and 24 is wider than might be assumed at a first glance. Both texts include: informal lexis, including slang expressions; scientific terms from the semantic field of nutrition; legal notices; instructions; **colloquial** expressions, etc. The following categories provide a way of identifying the range and variety of lexis found in any text. Judge particular words occurring in the texts against the scales of: Formal ....Informal Infrequent............................Frequent Archaic......................Recently coined Technical..............................Demotic
Semantics	Semantics is the study of the system of meanings carried by words and phrases and their combination in clauses and sentences.	Both texts use words and phrases to convey clear denotative meanings, but there are also words whose main purpose is to carry connotations that are positive, encouraging potential consumers to become customers. Such words are often imprecise: what, for example, does it mean to describe Salty Dog crisps as 'hand-cooked'?
Grammar	Words, phrases, clauses and sentences are grammatical units that combine to form texts which convey meaning. A text may be written or spoken. The simplest written texts may consist of a single word (e.g. 'STOP' on the road surface at a junction), but Samuel Richardson's novel Clarissa (1748) extended to nine volumes and over a million words. The grammar of a language consists of the rules and relationships that enable speakers and writers to combine words in order to construct and communicate meaning. **'Syntax'** is a term that is also used in this sense; 'morphology' is a term that refers to the changes in word forms, distinguishing tenses and other functions (e.g. swim … swimming … swam; child … children; possible … impossible).	In these texts, there are many distinct word, phrase and sentence elements. Text 23 contains phrases only on the front of the packet, rather than grammatically complete sentences, whereas Text 24 uses grammatically complete sentences in the short paragraph at the foot of the packet but phrases in the upper part of the packet front. For both texts the greatest grammatical variety occurs on the back of the packets.
Text structure	Texts that are clearly and effectively structured are likely to convey the writer or speaker's intended meanings accurately. *Coherent* texts convey a continuity of meaning that enables others to make sense of what writers or speakers intend. *Cohesion* is achieved by a range of techniques that establish links between different parts of the text, such as repetition and the use of synonyms, pronouns and ellipses.	Apparently simple texts such as those on snack food products are often the result of sophisticated and carefully crafted writing and design work. A key question is: do the various elements form an integrated whole, or is the impression one of disconnected snippets of text? The contrasts between humorous paragraphs and the legally necessary but arguably uninteresting lists of ingredients create particular difficulties for the writers and designers. How far do you think these Texts 23 and 24 have achieved effective integration of the contrasting elements that appear on the packets? For comparison, look at Text 25. Here the main text consists of two columns of narrative. Track the ways in which cohesion is achieved as the text moves from telling the story of 'That surprising Craig girl' to promoting a breakfast cereal.
Graphology and graphics	Graphology is the term that refers to the study of writing systems, including the use of fonts of different styles and sizes. Graphics refers more widely to the overall design of the texts including photographs, diagrams and other visual elements.	Design features are prominent elements of both crisp packet texts. The initial impact of the packets is largely achieved by visual design elements, but the main focus of your analysis of both texts should be on the ways in which language is used to fulfil the writers' intentions. You should also consider the relationship between the linguistic and visual aspects of the texts.

3 Informing and persuading

Key terms

Style: in written texts this is the choice and arrangement of words that create a particular effect. Jonathan Swift spoke of 'proper words in proper places'.

Critical response activity

1 Explain how the writer's judgements about purpose and audience affect the way the menu is written.

2 List the most striking and unusual phrases used in Text 14. Do they have anything in common?

3 Which dishes would you be most attracted to and which might put you off? Can you explain why you react as you do?

Informative writing deals with facts whereas persuasive writing aims to make us believe or do something. Text 15, for example, is clearly dealing with facts: it gives us details about hygiene regulations and it has no aim to persuade us, just to inform us about the law. It has the form of a factual document. Similarly Text 10 gives us lots of information about who eats tripe and how it is prepared. It is taken from a book in a series that deals with regional foods, so it is an extract from a lengthier form. Neither text is selling an idea or aiming to persuade us to think differently. However, 'Tripe' does include comments like 'a nourishing dish' and it mentions that it is 'a popular meal in hot weather'. There are some subtle hints that suggest the writer's positive views about tripe, but the primary purpose of the text is to inform rather than to persuade.

The distinction between information and persuasion is less clear in many texts. In this chapter, we look at four texts from the Anthology that provide information but also persuade us in different ways. We will consider form, purpose, audience and context and how these aspects affect the way the texts are composed. Reflecting on the composition can also involve analysing the structure as well as the expression or **style**. Some of the discussions are more detailed than others (Text 9 for example) but pointers are given to help you with your own thinking in some of the less detailed analyses (Text 13 for example). For some texts close scrutiny of the layout or any visual effects may be relevant too.

Text 14: A menu

Form, purpose, audience and context

The form here is clearly a menu that provides information about the food being served, but it also has an additional persuasive purpose: to entice us to buy. The layout of the menu is what we might expect in the context, with clearly divided sections making it easy to scan quickly. The menu is informative but it also attempts to persuade us by providing elaborate and tempting descriptions such as 'Roasted Yorkshire venison, spiced red cabbage, creamed potatoes with a braised faggot, juniper and thyme sauce'. Notice how the writer uses many premodifiers, to the extent that we often have to read several descriptors before we have any idea what is being offered, for example 'Braised High peak lamb breast', 'Oven roasted heritage beetroots' or 'Dark chocolate and malt whisky tart'. With its champagne list, its prices and dishes like 'Whole roast Cornish Mackerel', this is definitely not a fast food café. The intended audience are those interested in a place that uses locally sourced ingredients and they are prepared to pay premium prices for this. (Now see Critical response activity opposite.)

Commentary

1 A menu is intended to give information about the food on offer including prices, but it has a persuasive purpose too: to encourage the customer to order. The intended audience here are those who can afford to pay the prices and who are interested in food sourcing, and so the descriptions are detailed.

2 Phrases like 'Mixed leaf Chat Moss herb salad' seem mysterious. Is Chat Moss a place or a type of leaf? Other phrases such as 'Pressed

■ Practical activity

1 Collect several menus from different restaurants. You could look at the Ask or Prezzo chains (see Text 12), or a small independent café. Look at the language and answer the following questions:

a How clearly is the dish described?

b Is it made to sound appetising – and if so, how?

c Is the text informative or persuasive? Why is this approach taken?

2 Note some examples of descriptive phrases that are used (e.g. 'jus' instead of 'gravy'). Then answer the following questions:

a What image is the restaurant/café creating through its choice of language (e.g. sophisticated, fashionable, exotic, down-to-earth, or something else)?

b Would you be persuaded to eat one of the dishes?

terrine of partridge, rabbit and R.S. Ireland Bury black pudding' are strange combinations that are fascinating. Why 'pressed' and not shaped or flattened? Perhaps it is because the alliteration of pressed and partridge is more memorable. Throughout the menu the chef is clearly trying to advertise the regional sourcing of foods. But what most of the descriptions have in common is the use of sensuous detail to enable the reader to visualise, smell, taste and almost touch the food.

3 'Braised pigs head and warm cooking juices' could be off-putting because the inclusion of 'warm juices' connotes blood and is unappealing. To a vegetarian, 'Oven roasted heritage beetroots' appeals as it sounds as if it is wholesome and cooked traditionally.

(Everyone will respond differently to this question. Just ensure that you try to explain your response.)

■ Text 9: the Mail Online

Form, purpose audience and context

John Torode's text is the online version of an article originally published in the newspaper. The smiling image of Torode and the photograph of a woman about to tackle the meaty kebab are probably what we notice first, but the headline is also dominant and the clear purpose of the article is stated: 'Why we all need to eat red meat'. Notice the use of the inclusive pronoun 'we'. Torode speaks directly to his audience in an informal chatty way. This is an example of a text that is aiming to persuade us by using selective information which supports his views.

Structure

Torode structures the article very carefully in order to persuade us that his argument is valid. Look at the following activity which will help you to gain a clear overview of how he organises points.

■ Critical response activity

Answering the following questions will help you to focus closely on the text and will give you a clear overview of how Torode uses the information to support the case for eating red meat. (We will look at his use of language more closely in the next section.)

The table below contains some of the points that Torode makes in the first half of the article (Text 9). Copy the table and add your comments and reflections in the right-hand column. Some initial suggestions have been made for you. Look at the remainder of the article and add further examples and commentary to your table.

Main points	My thoughts
No decent meat in 1990	Torode's opinion, but seems to be overstated. Why would he want to exaggerate the difficulty in buying good-quality meat when he first arrived in Britain?
Chefs buying meat from France and Italy	General information (where does he get evidence?). Even if it were true for chefs, was it true for ordinary consumers?
Public worries about CJD and heart attacks	General hearsay – sweeping comment. Is he more interested in setting things up for his personal agenda than providing balanced comment?
Torode travels to find suppliers – opens restaurant	Personal actions – some self publicity
UN suggestion about cutting down on meat/worries about cholesterol	Uses factual information to give air of authority and leading to point that it is not beef's fault
But beef is not to blame – overeating is the problem. Other reasons to eat beef: proteins, monounsaturated fats, vitamins, trace minerals	Stresses beef is not at fault

Layout and presentation

The choice of font together with the use of photographs makes an impact on the reader. Analysing this visual impact is a useful exercise.

▓ Style

This is about the words that Torode chooses and their arrangement. In this section we will look at how appropriate and effective such a style is for his purpose and audience. You might find it useful to refer to lexis, register and rhetorical devices as well as other points. Simply identifying that Torode asks a question such as: 'What about the way the meat is produced – is there anything to fear?' is not helpful unless you explain the effect of the question. In this example he is making the point that we should dismiss as unfounded any fears we may have about meat production methods.

The linguistic and literary terms that are gradually being introduced to you are labels that will guide your thinking and suggest areas to focus on. Being familiar with some terms will provide you with a vocabulary to comment more sharply on extracts, but there is no substitute for individual, independent thinking. Feature-spotting is not enough; your focus should always be on the ways in which meanings are created in order to fulfil the writer's intentions.

Below are some working definitions for commonly used terms that are linked with the Torode article.

Lexis

Lexis is the vocabulary of a language. Notice how varied the lexis is. Look at how the author moves from colloquial expressions such as the imperative 'Well, calm down, everyone!' and phrases like 'chock-full' to more formal references to authority such as 'a Government veterinary body monitors any drugs'.

Register

In a written piece this refers to the level of formality or informality. Torode varies this to keep our interest, from the informal **monosyllabic lexis** associated with spoken discourse, to more elaborate noun phrases such as 'uninformed consumers' or 'public perception'. On the whole, however, we might say that he is trying to replicate real speech with its **exclamatives**, its chatty tone and inclusiveness.

Rhetorical devices

▓ Rhetorical question: a question that does not expect an answer but which stimulates thinking and draws the reader/listener in to the debate. Torode poses many questions to draw us into the discussion. For example: 'How much better to eat a simply grilled piece of well reared beef?'

▓ Repetition: used to reinforce a point. He repeats phrases for impact, such as 'too much' (for example: 'Too much fat, too much sugar, too much salt, too much everything').

▓ The power of three: grouping ideas (single words or phrases) into threes. See line 24: 'large, smoky, well marbled joint of beef', or the sentence 'The British public believed meat was expensive, tasteless but, worst of all, tainted with the risk of causing at least one life-threatening disease'.

▓ Critical response activity

What effect does each photograph in Text 9 have? Does the first one reinforce his points or not? What impact does the personal photograph have?

Look at the **typography** and the layout on the page. Notice the short paragraphs. What effect does that have on the reader? Is it easier to absorb and understand shorter sections? Do you get the impression of a person talking to you, moving backwards and forwards between topics in a rather loose and informal way?

▓ Key terms

Typography: the style and appearance of the print. This includes the kind of font chosen and its size and arrangement on the page.

Monosyllabic lexis: words made up of one syllable, e.g. cat, house, tune.

Exclamative: phrase or sentence that is an exclamation, e.g. 'What a mess!' or 'Never!'

Alliteration: the repetition of initial sounds such as in 'Full fathom five thy father lies'.

Hyperbole: exaggeration for effect, such as 'This pudding is sublime'.

Building to a climax or a surprising anticlimax: Torode gives details about his love affair with beef, including the opening of his restaurant. He balances this with a negative point of warning from the UN and then finally leads us to his blunt, dramatic conclusion: 'beef is not to blame'. (Notice also that the phrase is memorable because of the **alliteration** and the monosyllabic lexis.)

Hyperbole, or exaggeration: Torode uses sweeping statements such as 'Because we eat too much, full stop.' Or, 'Beef was the bad boy of British culture, but was it?'

Critical response activity

Having worked your way through the earlier activity on Text 9, answer the following question:

Bearing in mind the intended audience, how persuasive is Torode's article?

In your discussion look closely at:

- structure
- language choices
- Torode's use of anecdote
- Torode's use of dietary and scientific terms.

Text 13: Review of 'The Modern', in the Saturday magazine of the *Guardian*

Form, purpose, audience and context

Restaurant critics such as Michael Winner on the back page of the *Sunday Times* or A.A. Gill in the magazine sections often visit a restaurant, sample the food and then write a report. They give us information about their experience, but the success of the columns depends upon each writer establishing a clear persona (curmudgeonly critic or sophisticated, urbane gourmet) and giving us a very individual evaluation of the place and their meal. Text 13 in the Anthology is an example of this kind of restaurant review, which bluntly rates the Modern restaurant as '3 out of 10'. However, if you are looking for information about the meal you need to read the text closely. The form here is a journalistic review, but it does not set out specifically to inform. The purpose is more to entertain readers and show them that the writer is a discerning, interesting individual with a dry sense of humour. Compare this with Text 12 and its much shorter critiques that are not without humour but have a different audience and purpose. Text 13, however, does have persuasive powers; you would be unlikely to try the Modern restaurant after reading such a derogatory review!

Critical response activity

Use the following close analysis prompts to analyse Text 13. Make notes as you work through the points. The aim of the exercise is to get you to read closely and to think for yourself about what the writer is saying and how he shapes the text and selects his language for the intended audience: literate newspaper readers.

- **Informing:** how much information does the writer give you about the food and the restaurant? List the 'facts' that you can establish, e.g. it is at the top of the Urbis

building, it has a view, etc. Omit the evaluations and the opinionated descriptions such as his view of the restaurant as a 'chilly self-important horror' or 'corporate dining room chic that went out of fashion in 2003'.

- **Persuading:** list the kinds of phrases that convey the writer's strong opinions and attempt to persuade the reader to agree with him. For example, 'the last place on earth anyone vaguely sane would choose for their final meal'. Which words or phrases are particularly persuasive and why?

- **Personalisation and structure:** notice the way Norman frames his account with a personal story. Why does he do this and how effective is its use? Look closely at the opening, the narrative halfway through and the flourish of an ending.

- **Elaboration:** Norman uses concrete illustrations where possible to enliven the account. For example, when he speaks of the view, he does not just say it is 'hideous', but he suggests a far-fetched analogy between the cathedral and Natalie Portman, and the Premier Inn and Andrew Neil. What other examples can you find of such elaboration? Does it work? Are you interested enough in the images to want to read on?

- **Variety of lexis:** look at the variety of lexis in the article, from the colloquial 'This narrow space is done out' to the more exotic oxymoron of the 'sublimely charmless restaurant'. Or the use of clichés such as 'let's take a rain check on that' compared with the use of an obscure word like 'calumny'. What is the overall effect?

- **Engaging the reader:** how does the writer draw you in? Look, for example, at his use of first person and his rhetorical questions, e.g. 'Perhaps you have been obliged to park in the fast lane of the M6 during the rush hour?'

- **Syntax and grammar:** consider the sentence structure (syntax) and grammar. How varied is the sentence structure and with what effect? Look, for example, at the long opening sentence where the writer aims to puzzle and intrigue, and where he leaves the main declarative clause until the end – the assertion about how awful the restaurant is. Compare this with the shorter, more dramatic example: 'At £16.50, however, it was a calumny'.

- **Rhetorical devices:** analyse the techniques he uses from line 105 to line 128, the use of listing and repetition building up to an expectation of some climactic comment. In fact he ends with the bathos of 'the car not being worth the price of repairing'.

- **Successful:** assess how successful this piece of writing is. You will need to think about its purpose (to inform, persuade and to entertain) and whether the approach seems appropriate for the intended audience – weekend readers of the *Guardian*.

Text 11: The Vegetarian Society

Form, purpose, audience and context

This is in the form of a webpage so it is accessible to a wide audience. Its purpose is to give information and to appeal to potential vegetarian converts in a quietly persuasive way. As with Torode's article, it gives us some information and breaks it into 'seven simple steps' (a mildly memorable alliterative phrase).

Critical response activity

1. Using the same overview approach as you used for the Torode article, copy and complete the table about Text 11 that has been started below. This will provide you with a clear overview of the content. Focus on the main ideas of the piece and add your comments in the second column. You can add more examples and comments as your analysis of the webpage progresses.

Information	My comments
Mission statement: 'understanding and respect for **vegetarian lifestyles**'	Stressing concepts of understanding and respect suggest this is not going to be a tub-thumping persuasive piece. Has an air of quiet confidence.
Headline: 'Seven Simple Steps to Going – and Staying – Vegetarian'	Alliteration makes this memorable – but not 'hectoring'. Gentle sibilant sounds ('s' sounds) give this quiet appeal.
Stresses the importance of an individual and gradual approach to becoming a vegetarian	Simple advice expressed with a sincere tone created by the personal address: 'you', and the conditional opening: 'If it suits you'.

Key terms

Narrative: an account where events related (in speech or writing) are connected.

Analogy: another word for comparison.

Oxymoron: an expression that seems contradictory, e.g. 'living death'.

Rhetorical question: question that expects no answer from the listener or reader. It is often used as part of a persuasive strategy.

Declarative clause: a declarative clause is a statement that forms a section of a sentence, e.g. 'the pig is squealing'. (A clause contains at least a subject and verb, as shown here.)

Bathos: a change in mood, usually from the serious to the more mundane or trivial.

▶

Key terms

Key terms

Imperative: an utterance that has the power of an order, such as 'Write that essay now'.

Practical activity

It is interesting to rewrite a piece, adopting a different style. Go through this article and make it more assertive and dramatic, along the lines of the Torode piece. Alter the layout too and then annotate your new version identifying and explaining the changes you have made. Finally, write a short paragraph reflecting on the overall impact of the changes. You might like to consider how changing the style and layout affects our response, and whether the purpose and audience are now different.

Critical response activity *continued*

2   Now carry on analysing the article in this way. Focus on the style and give a detailed analysis of the following:

a   Syntax: the sentence structure. How varied is it?

b   Lexis and register: what kinds of words are used? How formal is the overall effect?

c   Persuasive techniques: what techniques are used to persuade the reader? Are there any rhetorical devices?

Here are just a few pointers about the types of sentences that might help you to get started:

The **imperatives** are gently expressed or mitigated, so the overall approach appears reasonable. For example, 'Try something new' or 'Learn a little about nutrition'. A bold imperative would be 'Study nutrition' or 'You must study nutrition'. Even the blunter 'Don't go it alone' does not shriek at the reader, but the intention of the order is to be supportive and helpful.

3   What impact does the layout and presentation have on you? Look at the photographs and their captions as well as the typography and the arrangement of the seven points.

4   Finally, answer the following questions:

a   How does the article signal its purpose and its intended audience?

b   Does the webpage achieve its purpose, in your view?

Comparing texts

An essential skill that is tested in the examination is that of comparing two texts. Before you can do this you need to be very familiar with the texts. Having closely examined Texts 9 and 11 you are now in a good position to compare them. A possible examination question based on the Anthology texts is shown below. The guidance points in the question are there to help you in framing your thinking. These are not prescriptive but are intended as helpful prompts to be applied when you judge them to be useful and relevant. They are explained in the annotations below.

Who has produced the article/text? What is its purpose? Who is receiving it (the audience)?

Compare two texts from the Anthology which present different views about what we should eat.

In your answer, write about some of the following where appropriate:

- *contexts of production and reception*
- *form and structure*
- *figurative language*
- *sound patterning.*
- *word choice*
- *grammar*
- *layout and presentation*

What kind of lexis is being used? Varied? Formal? Colloquial? Monosyllabic? Other?

This is a broad term that focuses on the way words are arranged and includes examining syntax.

The arrangement of text and visual material and the overall impact.

What form or genre is the text? (In this case they are both websites.) How is the text structured (the order of ideas and details; the sequence chosen) and with what effect?

Does the text contain language such as metaphors or similes? These are normally used to enliven a text. How do they affect our response? See Chapter 5 for more information.

Rhyme, or use of techniques such as alliteration.

Sample response: opening of a comparative essay

Both texts are extracts from websites: Text 9 is from the *Mail Online* and features a well-known chef, John Torode, speaking of the benefits of eating beef. Text 11, however, is from the Vegetarian Society and clearly has a different aim: to show the audience that becoming a vegetarian is a simple process. Both texts give us information: Text 9 speaks of health worries in beef eating (and refutes them) and Text 11 tells us about the Vegetarian Society and the help it offers. The main purpose of each article is similar – to persuade us that their views are apt and to convince us to join the vegetarian movement or to enjoy eating beef. But they each approach the topics very differently, even though the genre is similar.

> The opening paragraph sums up the main purpose of each text.

> Similarities are mentioned, such as genre and persuasive purpose.

> The final sentence hints at the direction of the next paragraph – talking about different approaches.

Torode states his views at the outset so there is no doubt about the direction of the article: 'Why we all need to eat red meat.' **On the other hand**, the Vegetarian Society (and there is no personal author named; the approach is to stress that this is a group) takes a simple, advisory approach, listing the stages a possible convert could follow. The seven points make it easy to digest and each section begins with a short sentence telling us about the content of the paragraph, for example, 'Learn a little about nutrition'. **The Torode piece** strikes the reader as a looser structure, made up of many short paragraphs, **with expressions that suggest a speaking voice (Well, calm down, everyone!).** The structure of Torode's argument is to deal with the bad publicity about beef eating and then refute this with information about the calorific value of other foods and compare this with beef. He also lists all of the nutrients which beef contains and leads up to a final assertion that meat is 'naturally healthy'. **There is structure to his piece, but it is** less obvious than the more business-like, segmented approach of the Vegetarian Society. The Torode article looks and sounds more like a newspaper columnist projecting his personality and distinctive opinions.

> By using phrases like these the writer moves smoothly between the two texts making comparative points.

> Supporting your points with quotations makes them more convincing and reasoned.

> The final two sentences sum up the general difference of approach. You could then continue with further comment on the layout and presentation before going on to unpick the style.

Practical activity

Now choose to write a response to one of the following questions:

1. Write an essay in answer to the question posed on page 22.

2. Answer the following question applying the same bullet points as used in the original question:

   Compare two texts that present information about restaurant experiences.

Whichever question you choose, make sure you use the prompts as a guide where relevant. Look back at the information on page 22 to refresh your understanding of them before you start to plan your essay. Think about the approaches shown in the sample opening to help you begin your own response.

Link

For more information on how to approach the examination questions, see Chapters 9 and 10.

Further reading

Crystal, D. (2004) *The Stories of English*. London: Penguin Books.

Flavell, L. and Flavell, R. (2006) *Dictionary of Idioms and their Origins*. London: Kyle Cathie Ltd.

Thorne, T. (2007) *Shoot the Puppy, A survival guide to the curious jargon of modern life*. London: Penguin Books Ltd.

This chapter covers:

- an introduction to the characteristics of spoken language

- learning how to analyse transcripts and the correct terminology to use

- close analysis of three spoken language texts from the Anthology: two examples of spontaneous dialogue, one example of a scripted monologue.

Practical activity

Speech and writing

- Interview a friend or family member and ask them to describe their favourite food, a favourite place, or a song. Listen carefully to how they talk. Jot down some of the phrases they use, or better still record the interview so that you can refer to it later. *If you plan to record them, make sure that they have given you their permission first.*

- Ask them to write down their views on the same topic. Compare their written account with the spoken one (as far as you are able) and make your own notes about any differences.

Key terms

Transactional talk: language that is used in 'transactions', such as when you are buying chocolate or arranging for a car service.

Phatic talk: social talk that helps to facilitate interactions, e.g. 'How are you?'

Introduction to spoken language

In our digital age, despite the increase in texting, emailing and posting on forums, most of us still spend more time talking and listening to speech (including radio and television) than we do writing or reading. Speech pre-dates any systematic writing systems and it is still, arguably, our main communicative channel. Even today in some societies, oral culture dominates and the vibrant tradition of storytelling, of weaving myths that entertain and advise, thrives. Where literacy skills are limited, a culture depends even more on the spoken word.

We vary the way we speak depending upon the context. In a situation such as social interaction with friends in a café, we are likely to choose an informal register. However, if we attend a job interview we are likely to use a more formal register. These are generalisations, of course, as people's expectations and approaches to situations differ. Studying spoken language of all kinds can help us to understand how different contexts influence language choices and how such choices create different meanings.

Transcripts are records of spoken language, transcribed with all of the characteristic features of spontaneous utterances preserved in print. The pauses, false starts, hesitations and repairs that we tend to ignore as listeners are recorded and these transcripts provide us with clear documents to study. They are not always easy to read as often we are given only a limited clue about the situation and we have to imagine the expressions and gestures, and discern the tone of the speech. But they are useful records that highlight how we speak and react in a variety of situations.

Text 19: A service encounter

Text 19 is a transcript of a simple situation: a dialogue between two friends choosing what to eat in an informal café. The waitress is quiet until line 16 where she answers questions, gives information and establishes how they want the food cooked. This is a clear example of **transactional talk** (the transaction is the purchasing of the food). There is also some **phatic talk**, for example the informal greeting, 'Hi', from the waitress or when S01 says 'you like mushrooms don't you?' Such talk helps to create and maintain the relationships between the speakers. Note that in transcripts the different speakers are usually denoted by S01, S02, etc.

Note that we know that S03 in Text 19 is a female because we are given the information on page 6 of the Anthology. However, be wary about making assumptions about the gender of speakers unless there is clear evidence.

Features of spoken language

The transcript contains many of the features that you will find in all kinds of speech (including Texts 17 and 18, which we will study later in this chapter). You will find some common features of spoken language listed in the table. (Note that the list is not exhaustive.)

Common features of spoken language

Characteristics of speech	Explanation	Some examples
Use of idioms and (depending upon context) more informal register	Informal lexis, especially in social interaction: use of slang, colloquialisms, dialect words and local expressions.	Simple lexis focuses on the food: 'Are the veggy burgers nice?' Semantic field of 'food' (words that are intrinsically connected to food): starter, barbecue sauce, etc. Informal: 'Yeah.'
Ellipsis	Grammatically incomplete sentences.	'Don't do cider, do you?'
Elision	Used to mimic natural shortened speech (when sounds are omitted from words or phrases), e.g. 'going to' is elided into 'gonna' and 'do not' becomes 'don't'.	'gonna have'
Non-fluency features	Hesitations, use of fillers such as 'you know' or voiced pauses 'erm, er'. These are often called **repairs and reformulations**.	'Erm' and 'er' are used as hesitations (that occur naturally when choosing food). There are also many self-corrections/repairs: 'Er, d'you have, er have you got pineapple juice?'
Back channel behaviour	Providing feedback – letting the listener know you are paying attention.	'Oh right' (line 4), 'Yes' (line 28).
Tag questions	A question usually added to a declarative statement to make it interrogative. A technique often used to draw in a speaker.	'you like mushrooms, don't you?' (line 13).
Use of discourse markers	Words and phrases such as 'so', 'all right then', 'now', 'well'. They mark the boundaries between topics.	'All right' (line 33).
Overlapping and interruptions	Dialogue that overlaps or is spoken simultaneously.	'Mm, are you gonna have a starter, what you gonna have?' (line 6) and 'Yeah … I'm trying not to have nachos' (line 7).
Use of deixis	When 'shorthand' references are made to ideas or objects that the speakers understand. For example: 'I will buy the shoes at that shop over there.' (The shop is not named.)	'A veggy one' is shorthand for veggy burger – but the participants understand what is being talked about (line 5).

Key terms

Idiom: expression that is often informal and figurative and is regularly used by a distinct group of people (such as English speakers in England), which outsiders might have difficulty interpreting at first. For example 'spill the beans' or 'the sky's the limit'.

Elision: when sounds are omitted from words or phrases, such as 'don't' instead of 'do not'.

Repairs and reformulations: when a speaker makes corrections to their own speech. For example, a speaker says: 'He, no she, walked into the room, or rather staggered slowly.' The speaker repairs (corrects) and changes the pronoun from he to she and then reformulates by altering the verb and qualifying it.

Tag question: a question usually added to a declarative statement to make it interrogative.

Discourse marker: word or phrase that marks the boundary between topics.

Deixis: when 'shorthand' references are made to ideas or objects that the speakers understand. For example: 'I will buy the shoes at that shop over there' (the shop is not named).

Context dependent: word choice that varies depending upon the situation. For example, you will speak differently when asking for directions from a stranger compared with asking a close friend for a favour.

Schema: a set of expectations in a given situation. For example, when attending a job interview there is a schema (an expected framework) that will influence what you do and say.

How we speak is very **context dependent**. This means that it varies depending on where we are, who we are with and what the expectations of us are in any given situation. This encounter follows the typical **schema** of a service encounter. As mentioned above, there is a little phatic talk as the two friends choose their food. The waitress is fairly taciturn too. Look at her elliptical question, 'What cheese?' rather than

Critical response activity

Copy the table on page 25, omitting the middle column. Then add your own examples from Text 19 to those already given in the column 'Some examples'. You will now have a more detailed summary of the spoken language features in this text.

Key terms

Paralinguistic feature: sound that is used in addition to or alongside the language system, e.g. grunt, cough, laugh, and aspects of voice quality such as intonation, pitch, loudness and speed.

Agenda setting: the 'setting' or choice of a topic for a conversation or interaction.

the fuller, 'What cheese would you like?' This is followed by an equally brief question, 'What's the difference?' S01 does not spell out the sense fully, but in the situation the waitress understands the request.

This links to pragmatics, which is concerned with assessing the meaning that an utterance has in a particular context. We often depend upon knowledge of the context in which words are spoken to be able to fully grasp what is implied. If you overhear someone saying 'that's very late' and you have not heard any of the rest of the conversation it would be difficult to know what is going on. Is it a late delivery of a parcel; the late arrival home of a son or daughter; the late blooming of a flower? Without the surrounding context the meaning remains ambiguous.

Paralinguistic features

The Greek word 'para' means 'by the side of', so paralanguage is the sounds that are used in addition to or alongside the language system. For example grunts, coughs, laughs and aspects of voice quality such as intonation, pitch, loudness and speed. Such sounds can all contribute to the overall mood and atmosphere of the situation. But we have to deduce the **paralinguistic features** in Text 19. For example, look at 'Sorry', said by the waitress in line 18. It could be said in so many different ways, but examining the context reveals that she has either not understood or not heard the question about the cider, or maybe she is shaking her head implying 'Sorry, no'. There will always be ambiguous moments in transcripts. Without the visual recording of the scene we can only offer probable interpretations.

Body language

This term is often linked with paralinguistics and it refers to bodily behaviour: stance, gestures, expressions, eye contact and movement. Most transcripts do not indicate these, so we are very dependent on a close scrutiny of the language in order to draw our conclusions.

In any interaction speakers may take turns to speak. Some may dominate and have lengthier and more numerous turns, or they may determine the topic (**agenda setting**) and the direction of the conversation or discussion. Look, for example, at how S01 leads the way and S02 follows, using the tentative question 'Can I have?', or softening requests with '*I think* I'm gonna have'.

Critical response activity

1. Read Text 19 aloud, taking separate parts if possible.

2. Using the common features of speech table (see page 25) work your way through the text, making notes in answer to the following questions:

   a. Identify and list the striking speech features, such as informal lexis.

   b. Track the number of turns each speaker takes and who leads the way at different points.

3. Analyse the context:

   a. How does the situation influence the way the speakers act and what they say? What are our expectations of the encounter?

   b. Examine the roles that each speaker takes: how do they talk to each other and how do they react to each other? Is this what you might expect? Does anything surprise you?

4. Now, use your notes to help you answer the following question:

   Analyse the transcribed encounter between two friends and a waitress in an informal restaurant, focusing on the linguistic interaction.

   - Write three or four paragraphs in answer to the question.
   - Refer closely to the text.
   - Begin with an overview of the scene.
   - You could then comment on how the context influences the interaction, looking in detail at the way the participants interact and at what meets your expectations and what (if anything) surprises you.
   - Guidance on how to start your analysis is given in the following commentary.

Commentary

Here is a sample first paragraph and part of the second paragraph to get you started.

> Text 19 is a scene that is set in an informal restaurant where two friends are ordering food. It is a service encounter: two speakers decide what to order, ask the waitress for extra information and finally make their decisions. The encounter ends with a polite but informal 'thanks'. Everything remains focused on food choices.
>
> The context influences the action. There is transactional talk in a café where the transaction is the purchasing of food. We can tell, however, that the two speakers know each other due to the use of such phatic phrases as the tag question 'you like mushrooms, don't you?'. Also, the language is informal 'gonna; yeah' and the speech overlaps at times. The register of the encounter between all three speakers is informal. For example, the waitress's casual 'Hi' is spoken at the same time as S02's musings about what to drink.

Text 18: A family meal

This transcript shows the interaction between family members when a meal is being served. It is a domestic setting, very different from the public context of Text 19. But it is not as easy to understand as Text 17. There are references to issues that we have no knowledge of, and there are hints of tension. It is difficult to be exact about the sense at times, for example in the sentence, 'I would rather do it'. Is the pronoun 'it' referring to the serving of chilli or is it referring to the issue he is discussing with his mother? Also, there are phrases that seem ambiguous initially, such as 'I don't see any others'. Does this refer to other people or other bits of food? However, when the rest of the extract is digested it appears that he is talking about bags of chips.

As an outsider (not a family member) it is not easy to assess the sense or tone of Text 18, especially without the help of paralinguistics and body language. Single words can hold semantic difficulties, for example 'this' in 'Now this isn't according to grandpa now' (line 16). The pronoun could have myriad meanings: it could refer to a recipe or a way of serving the meal or something else entirely. We can look at the pragmatics, at the context of the declarative sentence, to assess the meaning, but there will still be different interpretations of the sense. We would need to be there to hear the sarcasm or detect the impatience. So a transcript highlights how meanings are so context dependent and how, with only speech to assess, conclusions about the nature of interactions will always be tentative.

Text 17: A transcript from the BBC programme *Nigella Express*

Analysing monologues

We have looked at scenes where people are interacting through dialogue and where there are some unspoken rules of cooperation such as taking turns to speak. In a monologue, however, one speaker dominates. The speaker could be telling a story, giving instructions, doing stand-up comedy or making a speech. Successful monologues will connect with their listeners and draw them into the story or convince them about the points expressed or, in the case of Text 17, entertain and inform, and show the viewer how to make Mexican scrambled eggs.

Practical activity

Making your own transcripts

Record a small group discussion, or an interview or a radio programme that contains spontaneous talk. If you set up a discussion amongst a group of friends provide a stimulus for talk: a newspaper article or a controversial topic. Or one person could lead with some simple questions about opinions on the value of travel, or the impact of YouTube, or the rise in university fees. The idea is to get everyone talking naturally and enable them to forget they are being recorded. The transcripts can then be used for analysis.

Note: the speakers can remain anonymous but they must still give their permission before the transcripts can be used by anyone else.

Practical activity

Text 18 is an interesting text to dramatise and it is certainly easier to understand the meaning if different voices are used. If you perform it you should become aware of how the talk is linked with the action of serving the meal. You will also notice some of the typical features of spoken language (mentioned in the table on page 25). The family members do not need to explain points to each other, so there is much ellipsis and deixis.

Practical activity

1 Record a three-minute section from a cookery demonstration programme. Make a transcript of this and then analyse its features. Consider the kinds of lexis and expressions used and think about how effective the overall style of the broadcast is, bearing in mind audience and purpose.

2 Compare the approach (the lexis, the structure, the talking to camera) with that of Text 17. Which do you think is the most interesting and which would persuade you to try out the recipe? Is the most entertaining commentary always the most persuasive?

Further reading

- Cockcroft, S. (1999) *Investigating Talk*. London: Hodder and Stoughton.
- Crystal, D. (1998) *Language Play*. London: Penguin Books Ltd.
- Matthews, P. H. (2007) *Oxford Concise Dictionary of Linguistics*. Oxford: Oxford University Press.
- Pridham, F. (2002) *The Language of Conversation*. London: Routledge.

The recipe for the dish is given in Text 16 and it is introduced by the presenter who asserts that this is a wonderful 'hangover cure'. Nigella is probably reading from a teleprompt, but there are spontaneous moments too. She creates a persona who seems human, who might be 'tempted' to go to a party just so that she can 'whip' up this dish the next day. (A little far-fetched, but an attempt to enliven the facts of the recipe.)

Critical response activity

1 In Text 17, what techniques and emotions does Nigella use to draw in the listener/viewer?

2 What features of spoken language help to make this sound natural?

3 Nigella is very expressive and evaluative. What effect does this have on the listener? Give some other examples.

4 The lexis is varied. Give some examples, and comment on the effect of such variety.

5 What is the main aim of a demonstration like this and how do you respond to her approach?

Commentary

1 She gives personal details about her life (what she feels like in the morning), creating the fiction that she is confiding in the viewer. The viewer is a friend whom she addresses as 'you', 'let me tell you' and she gives gentle advice, 'don't be hard on yourself'.

2 Spoken language features include: discourse markers such as 'now', 'well', 'anyway'; informal expressions like 'ok'; the use of asides, introducing extra details during the demonstration such as 'normally I'd be making toast'; the use of elision, 'I'm gonna'.

3 Her approach can seem like an elaborately staged performance because there are so many hyperbolic expressions: 'I love', 'I feel', 'perfection'. But she does connect with the audience. She uses the first person pronoun 'I' throughout and we hear about her worries, her hopes, her likes and dislikes.

4 The lexis varies from simple phrases like 'I'm making it because I love it' to the crafted 'a first thing frittata party' with its alliterative effect. The climactic ending 'oh the softness of this golden egg against the crispness of the golden tortilla' seems scripted, as does an elevated phrase like 'syncopated move'. However, the variety of lexis is entertaining and she is able to conjure up images in the viewer's mind to 'sell' her recipe.

5 The aim is to entertain, inform and to give us some instruction on how to make this recipe. Whether she succeeds depends upon our reaction to her (invented?) persona: party loving and excitable and very enthusiastic about food. Her seductive tones and exclamations 'oh' and 'ah' can amuse or irritate, but undoubtedly she tries to connect with the viewer and to make the whole process appear spontaneous and enjoyable.

Literary language, fiction and audience

Think about it

Ernest Hemingway wrote movingly and graphically in a deliberately childlike way. For example, look at his short story 'Indian Camp' first published in a 1925 collection *In Our Time*. The sentences are simple, the lexis is basic and the descriptive detail is minimal.

Link

Look back at the section on paralinguistics on page 26. Notice how Galsworthy conveys a speaker's tone by referring to 'murmured' or 'cried scornfully'. The mood is created not just by the dialogue but by authorial comments on the ways of speaking (or remaining silent).

Writing for a specific audience

We usually adapt what we write or say to suit our audience, or we risk having no audience or listeners at all. Think of a very simple plot for a children's story: a young girl finds a hedgehog trapped in wire netting; other children come to help with the rescue; other animals come to watch; adults are not involved; the child feeds the hedgehog and then frees it in the woods. It is such a simple, cosy story with a successful outcome, but it has to be brought to life for its audience. The writer could use vivid, colourful descriptions with references to sounds, movements and actions, with much repetition for emphasis. This would encourage the child to actively respond to the story and to enjoy matching the words with the illustrations.

If you take the same story line for adult fiction, there might seem to be little of interest. To successfully engage the audience the writer would need to focus on the nature of the child and their relationship with the group of helpers. The story would need to be adapted for an adult audience, with a more complex plot and more detailed reflections about character. However, the lexis might still be simple. Just because the story is written for an adult audience, it does not mean that the sentences have to be complex and the sense convoluted.

The literary language of fiction

In this chapter we are looking at the literary language of stories, which is a hugely varied topic. But what most successful literature has in common is an ability to draw readers into a story, to entice them to 'turn the page' and discover how the plot is finally resolved. A writer does this through careful choice of lexis and careful arrangement of ideas and descriptions, and so creates a style or a mode of expression that is appropriate to the story and appeals to the audience. This expression can be elaborate: look at the long, complex sentences in Text 29 *The Warden* by Anthony Trollope. The author describes, in minute detail, the 'well-furnished breakfast parlour' with its 'thick, dark, costly carpets'. Or expression can be simple, as shown in the short sentences in Text 31 *The Man of Property* by John Galsworthy. Tension is created by what is unspoken: 'long silence followed' and 'there was a lengthy pause' or 'no one replied'. The interaction at the table seems on the surface humdrum, but the writer hints throughout at the undercurrents of feeling.

Children's literature is often seen as a separate genre of fiction, but to be successful, the same point applies: the child has to become engrossed in the story, it has to come alive in their imagination.

Text 30: *Little Grey Rabbit's Pancake Day*

This is an illustrated children's story, which could be read aloud to a very young child or given to an older one to read for themselves. The animal characters are easily identifiable in the illustrations and the story is simple, humorous and has a happy ending. Pancakes are made, tossed, eaten and the day ends with a song that a child could sing along with.

It has all of the ingredients for a successful children's story and it has remained popular since it was first published.

Context of production

Background information

- Alison Uttley (1884–1976) was brought up in rural Derbyshire.
- She was one of the first few female physics graduates at Manchester University.
- After her husband died she needed to support herself and her son, which gave her the incentive to begin writing children's stories.

Critical response activity

Read Text 30 aloud several times. This will make you more aware of the dialogue, the different voices and of how well suited the story is for the intended audience. Then make notes about the following aspects. Complete your notes before looking at the possible responses and advice given in the commentary below. Make sure that you always support your ideas and conclusions by using evidence from the text.

1 The narrative structure:

   a Examine the syntax of the sentences: are the points easy to follow?

   b Does she vary the kinds of sentences used? What is the effect of this?

   c How is the whole text structured (the sequence of events)?

You might find it useful to use a tabular approach for this analysis. The table below has been provided as an example. Copy it and add an extra column to record your evaluation of the effects of Uttley's choices. Continue recording the information in your own table by adding further examples and comments. This will provide you with a clear idea of the order of action as well as an awareness of the impact of different sentence types on the reader. Be aware that Uttley's sentence structure is often more complex and varied than it appears at first.

Key terms

Simple: a simple sentence contains at least one subject and one verb, for example, 'I cycled'. Or the sentence can have an object; e.g., 'I' (subject) 'bought' (verb) 'a new bicycle' (object).

Compound: a compound sentence contains more than one clause linked with a connective word such as 'but' and 'and'; e.g., 'I bought a new bicycle *and* I cycled home'.

Complex: a complex sentence includes one or more subordinate clauses; e.g., 'I bought a new bicycle, *which was very expensive*, and I cycled home'.

Paragraphs – summary of each	Examples of sentence structures used
The clever rabbit's method of pancake making and tossing it. A detailed description.	Mostly **simple** and **compound**, but with use of reporting clauses such as 'warned Grey Rabbit'.
Onlookers' reactions and rabbit's comments.	See above.
Pancake lands on hare's head – amusing scene.	Compound and **complex** (e.g. there is a subordinate adjectival clause 'the batter, *which was ready in the bowl*').

2 Visual impact:

   a What are the features that strike you?

   b Does the layout and presentation seem apt for a young child?

3 The language used:

   a What kind of lexis and descriptive detail does she use?

   b Do her choices seem appropriate for the audience?

   c Does she engage the listener/reader effectively?

Commentary

1   *The narrative structure*. Using a table as suggested will provide you with some detailed notes, so you can then write a fuller answer than the summary given here. In particular you can examine specific compound and simple sentences, assessing how well they convey the story.

Brief summary

The narrative is straightforward. It moves from how to make a pancake, to an amusing incident with the hare and then the fox, to more pancakes being made by Moldy Warp and Fuzzypeg. It finishes with Grey Rabbit making the last pancake and sharing it with Fuzzypeg. The final song is sung while the other animals tidy the house and wash up. The sentence structure is often compound, where clauses are linked with conjunctions in a simple sequencing of ideas. Compound sentences enable the listener to follow the action easily. The range of connectives used in the sentences is limited to 'but', 'and' and 'that'. The lexis is kept simple for the target audience. However, Uttley does use complex sentences, such as 'He put an extra egg in it, which he had found, and a pinch of honey and a sprinkle of wild thyme'. But there is only one **subordinate clause** used here ('which he had found'). Excessive use of subordinate clauses might make it difficult for a child to follow the action. Uttley's use of complex sentences is limited, but their inclusion does add variety.

> ■ Key terms
>
> **Subordinate clause:** a clause (which usually contains a subject, verb and object) that gives additional information to the main clause, and is subordinate to it. For example, 'I bought a new bicycle (main clause), which was very expensive (subordinate adjectival clause, describing the bicycle).

2   *Visual impact*. Here are some notes on features that are striking. However, your list is likely to be different and more detailed. For example, there are only brief comments on two of the illustrations. You will need to have examined each one carefully.

■ Paragraphs: separate, well-spaced out paragraphs are less daunting for children to read than an unbroken page of text. This story is divided into relatively short paragraphs and short lines.

■ Font: the blue font is interesting but it is difficult to conclude what impact it has. Perhaps it is intended to reflect the colourful, imaginary world.

> Notice here that this comment is qualified with 'Perhaps' and it is tentative. It is better to do this rather than to assert a simple conclusion for which you have no evidence.

■ Illustrations: the pictures complement the story well, for example the first one clearly illustrates the pancake tossed by Little Grey Rabbit and caught by Hare. The illustrations also reinforce the mood and the story line. The pastel colours are gentle and the world created seems safe and cosy. The child can make sense of the scene and assess the characters' expressions and roles. For example, the final domestic scene shows Fuzzypeg and Little Grey Rabbit framing the fireplace and eating their pancakes contentedly.

3   *The language*.

Uttley uses many monosyllabic (one syllable) but **dynamic verbs** such as 'beat', 'tossed', 'ran', 'threw', 'leap' and 'grabbed'. The effect is to create movement and to make us aware of the action. There is much repetition, for example 'tossed', and phrases like 'made the *last* pancake with the *last* scrap of egg and the *last* scraping of flour', which helps the new reader to become familiar and confident with particular words.

> ■ Key terms
>
> **Dynamic verb:** verb that refers to movement or action, such as run, leap, grasp.

The premodification is kept simple and usually limited to one or occasionally two adjectives such as 'little', 'extra' and 'neat little'. She uses the occasional more striking adjective such as 'golden', 'wild' or 'clever' to add colour and variety. Lengthier descriptive phrases are used which help the reader to visualise the scene, such as 'a brush made of birch twigs' or 'sorrel juice squeezed from the wild wood-sorrel leaves'. In fact, the first long paragraph contains much detailed description of pancake making and uses words that would extend the vocabulary of a child, as well as vividly conjuring up the scene in all its colour and movement. The eggs were beaten until they 'frothed' and the mixture is described as 'bubbling and spreading' over the pan. The description of raising the edges with 'a thin, little stick' is very effective as the reader can imagine the action. Then the reference to 'a sudden jerk of her paw' is a concrete detail that exactly captures the tossing movement.

So, there is a balance between descriptive detail about how the pancakes are made (mostly in the opening paragraph), with clear actions described ('he tossed so hard the pancake went over the hedge into the field'). Direct speech is used too and this allows the reader to hear the animals' voices, visualise their reaction, and discern their different characteristics. Additionally, Uttley uses rhyme in the final song, which reiterates some of the lexis used earlier and provides a conclusion to the story that is enjoyable to read aloud.

Her style is appropriate for a young audience. There is variety in the expressions and in the actions described, but there is always momentum in the story. It moves at a fast pace with just the right amount of repetition, and the right amount of colourful detail to avoid any tedium. There is plenty for the listener to remember and repeat; and the child reading it will gain confidence and be stretched by the fresher, low-frequency words used ('snippet', 'sprinkled' and 'muttering'). Uttley engages the reader effectively, with an accessible, well-illustrated story that contains an interesting mixture of dialogue and descriptive detail.

Practical activity

1. Try rewriting the third and fourth paragraphs of Text 30 using more complex sentences. What is the effect on the listener/reader?

2. Gather a selection of two or three illustrated children's stories. Analyse each along the lines of the Uttley analysis, looking at the language, the structure and the visual impact. In your view, which story has the most appeal for its intended age group? Make sure you can justify your conclusions with evidence.

3. Write a **pastiche** of the Uttley extract. A pastiche imitates the style of an existing text, often for gently comedic effect. It imitates the features such as sentence structure and **narrative sequence**, but alters the content. So your pastiche could be a short story about a child making fairy cakes, or a talking giraffe meeting a crocodile. Writing a pastiche should help you to become more familiar with how a text is created and structured.

Key terms

Pastiche: an imitation of the style of a text.

Narrative sequence: the order in which a story is told.

■ Text 28: *Oliver Twist* by Charles Dickens

Context of production

Text 27 provides useful information about workhouse diets and it helps us to understand the context of production for Dickens' novel *Oliver Twist.* Furthermore, the haunting illustration of Oliver famously asking for 'more' helps the reader to visualise the conditions and the situation. In addition to the tabular information about diet, we are told how the novel was first published – it was serialised in monthly instalments, running from 1837 to 1839. That was a long time to keep readers interested, but Dickens was a master at handling multiple plot lines, at ending episodes with cliffhangers and keeping the readers in suspense and eager for the next episode. In essence, Dickens was providing soap opera for 19th-century readers, but it is entertainment with an edge as the novels are full of social criticism. Text 27 accurately depicts the workhouse with its meagre diets and authoritarian regime. But the serial magazine publication and the subsequent publication as a novel would not have been a success if this work were simply a **diatribe** about conditions in workhouses, and an exposure of social evils in the Victorian age. It has a compelling narrative and characters that engage us, and it is these qualities that often make a fictional text successful.

■ Research point

It can help you to appreciate and understand a text better if you know some details about the writer's background and the social and historical context of its production. A starting point for Dickens could be one of these websites:

■ www.dickensmuseum.com

■ http://charlesdickenspage.com

■ http://dickens2012.org.

■ Key terms

Diatribe: a bitter condemnatory written or spoken attack, denouncing an idea or person.

■ Critical response activity

Make notes in answer to the following questions before you read the commentary below.

1 Narrative structure: examine the order of events and the details that Dickens gives us. This will give you a clear overview of the text.

2 Narrative voice: how is the story told? Is it first person, for example 'I stared' etc.? Or is it third person, for example 'he stared' etc.? How does the method affect our reactions?

You might find it useful to make notes using a table like the one below. Copy the table and add your own detail about the narrative structure in the left-hand column. You could add some of your own reflections in the 'Initial thoughts' column as well. Then you can refer back to these when you answer the question about how Dickens brings the scene to life (in the next Critical response activity).

Summary	Initial thoughts
Section 1, paragraph 1: description of the hall; details of the 'slow starvation'; they draw lots and Oliver is to be the spokesperson to ask for more.	Scene setting: giving details of their usual diet and then building up to the choice of Oliver as spokesman.
Section 2, paragraph 2: the evening when Oliver will speak. The scene is set and tension builds.	A contrast in style: a dramatic section.
Section 3, the incident: the master's reaction and then reactions from the board.	A combination of descriptive detail and speech, ending with the climactic, melodramatic 'that boy will be hung'.

Commentary

1 *The narrative structure.* The sequence is carefully structured, building up tension from the initial lengthy descriptions of the diet and the striking image of the bowls being licked so clean they never needed washing, to the amusing but shocking image of a boy who might turn into a cannibal, such is his hunger. Dickens then builds tension

■ **Key terms**

Linear narrative: a storyline where events clearly follow in chronological sequence.

Omniscient narrator: the storyteller (the author) has a complete knowledge of all characters and all situations. The story is presented using the third person (he/she/it) rather than the first person method (I).

■ **Think about it**

What difference does it make to the reader if the story is told by an 'omniscient narrator' or if it is told through the eyes of a character? Find two short stories that take a different narrative approach and compare them, thinking about the advantages and disadvantages of each method.

further with the sense of slow motion: 'a long grace was said'. There is much nudging and whispering before Oliver finally stands. The final section enables the reader to imagine these board members with all their lack of feeling and understanding: their 'horror' at someone daring to want more to eat. The master is appalled and flummoxed because Oliver has spoken up. The reader would want to read on to find out what actually happens. This is a **linear narrative**, taking the reader sequentially from the choice of lots, to Oliver's speech and then the reactions.

2   *The narrative voice.* The story is not told by Oliver, but by Dickens as the **omniscient narrator**. As such, he can select and focus on any aspect of the story. He takes control and he has complete knowledge of all characters and all situations. For example, Dickens reveals Oliver's state of mind as 'desperate with hunger and reckless with misery'. He describes the room and selects the details that support the picture of somewhere functional and bleak: 'a large stone hall with a copper at one end'. As readers, we have access to information that is denied to the characters, so whilst Oliver and the inmates do not hear the Board's comments, we (the readers) are given a full picture.

So this method enables the author to focus on the whole scene. The events are not viewed just through Oliver's eyes and the author can describe scenes and comment on emotions that Oliver may not have experienced. The author behaves like a roving cameraman, moving between characters and scenes, selecting some elements to focus on and ignoring others. He is choosing elements that will help to convey his viewpoint and will further the plot.

Dickens' style

Style is a broad term that covers everything about word choice, arrangement and the resultant tone and mood created by the writer. It is a vast area and it can often be difficult to know how or where to start an analysis. We might say that Dickens is a master at bringing a scene to life so that the reader easily visualises the scene and characters and feels the emotions conveyed. However, these are generalisations and we need to be more specific. How exactly does Dickens achieve this?

■ **Critical response activity**

Answer the following question using the prompts and hints:

How does Dickens bring to life the scene in Text 28?

Examine the details that enable us to imagine the scene and the characters.

What is the effect of using direct speech?

Approaching this question:

■ **Option 1:** Start at the beginning and work chronologically through the piece making your notes. List the features that are foregrounded (most noticeable) and consider their effect and how they compare or link with other sections of the text. For example, you might note the simple, clear description of the dining room, with the two monosyllabic

premodifiers 'large stone'. You could then note that this introduction is very different to the more animated second paragraph where the use of active verbs creates more drama.

■ **Option 2:** Group together all comments about lexis, all comments about syntax, etc. You can use the prompts that will be given in the examination paper (see Chapter 3, page 22) as a framework for your notes.

Whichever approach you choose, there will always be overlaps. For example, writing about lexis might involve analysing types of verbs used. This could lead to a discussion of a particular sentence structure, and then to how tension is created. Look at the second paragraph with its emphasis on verbs: 'evening arrived' and 'gruel was served out'. You will see how choice of lexis, especially excessive use of verbs arranged in short clauses, helps to build tension and to evoke the scene vividly.

Commentary

Dickens varies the lexis from more elaborate phrases such as 'festive composition', 'public rejoicing' and 'solemn conclave' to simple but evocative descriptions such as 'large stone hall' or 'fat, healthy man'. The more elaborate lexis is sometimes used when the author is being critical and **satirical**. For example, the scene with the women ladling out gruel is anything but a 'festive composition', it is the opposite. This is an example of Dickens' **irony**. Similarly the critical tone of the author is conveyed in phrases like 'on occasions of great public rejoicing' when all they are given is 'two ounces and a quarter of bread besides'. We expect them to receive much more than these rations. Dickens' tone is mocking. He also uses exaggeration, or hyperbole, to emphasise certain points, for example 'the assistants were paralysed with wonder; the boys with fear'. Notice the balanced sentence and the use of **antithesis** for dramatic effect. This is **figurative language** as well, although we would normally expect the collocation 'paralysed with fear' to be used. Dickens subverts (undermines) our expectations for dramatic impact.

Dickens uses precise descriptive detail to evoke a scene. The image of the 'polished spoons' and the haunting picture of the boys who 'sit staring at the copper' is memorable. There are many examples of this kind of detail, such as the adjectival phrase 'wild with hunger' or the balanced phrases 'desperate with hunger' and 'reckless with misery' (**parallelism**) that exactly sum up Oliver's mood. In addition, Dickens makes effective use of dynamic verbs to move the story along. This is particularly noticeable in the second paragraph where noises and movements are emphasised, such as 'stationed', 'winked', 'nudged' and 'whispered'. They are not dramatic movements or noises, but they lead up to Oliver's plea and the subsequent 'stupefied astonishment of the master'. The actions of the master are then emphasised with 'aimed a blow' and the verbs 'pinioned 'and 'shrieked'.

Using direct speech often brings a scene to life. The master's exclamation 'What!' and the detail of it being said in a 'faint voice' convey his reactions exactly. Limbkins' horror and his use of formal register, 'the supper allotted by the dietary', highlight the complete lack of understanding amongst this 'conclave'. The small detail of the white waistcoat is sufficient to hint at the kind of person on the board and the ridiculous overreaction, 'he must hang', emphasises their unforgiving attitudes.

So this is storytelling that engages the reader, describes the scene and mood and also makes us aware of the authorial viewpoint. We discern that Dickens disapproves of the organisation of the workhouse and the treatment of its inmates.

Key terms

Satirical: writing in a satirical way involves adopting a mocking tone, but with serious undertones. Dickens mocks (satirises) the treatment of workhouse inmates, with the serious intent of drawing the reader's attention to the problems.

Irony: when a writer deliberately says one thing and means something else. For example, 'He was a very generous man and in his will he left his only sister his least-valuable stamp collection'. From this we can infer that he was the opposite of generous.

Antithesis: when opposing ideas or images are used for effect, for example: 'Man proposes; God disposes'.

Figurative language: this extends and alters the literal meaning of words. We might speak of someone having a 'sunny nature'. There is an implied comparison between their attitude and the brightness of the sun, but we do not assume the person has the qualities of the sun itself. The purpose of using figurative language in real talk or in fiction is to enable us to perceive something more vividly or allow us greater insight into a character or story.

Parallelism: when similar grammatical constructions are used and placed next to each other (in parallel). For example 'a sharpening wind, a blackening sky'.

■ Comparing literary texts: Text 28 (*Oliver Twist* by Charles Dickens) and Text 29 (*The Warden* by Anthony Trollope)

■ Critical response activity

Compare Text 28 (an extract from *Oliver Twist*) with Text 29 (an extract from *The Warden*) looking particularly at narrative voice and authorial viewpoint, and the different ways in which each writer brings the scene to life.

(Narrative voice refers to the distinctive manner or expression of the narrator of the story. This can be a character's voice or the author's voice or a mixture of the two. Authorial viewpoint is linked with this as we discern the overall attitudes of an author from the way the story is told.)

This will give you practice at grouping ideas and marshalling your thoughts to create a coherent comparison.

Make a plan for your answer first. It should include the following:

■ An overview of content: comparing purpose and audience and the effect of this on the content.

■ Similarities including discussion of lexis, descriptive detail and any figurative language, or techniques such as use of alliteration or **onomatopoeia**, syntax and sentence types.

■ Differences including discussion of lexis, descriptive detail, and any figurative language, or phonological techniques, syntax and sentence types.

■ Authorial viewpoint (you may have mentioned this earlier, but gather your thoughts here).

■ Conclusions: include some opinion on how effective each passage is, in your view, together with your explanation.

Now, write the answer in continuous prose.

■ Key terms

Onomatopoeia: words that sound like their meaning. For example 'slush', 'snap' or 'crisp'.

Commentary

Here are some opening paragraphs for such a comparison. Notice that right from the start the reader is being alerted to comparative points. This first paragraph includes a brief overview and comparison of the content of each extract, together with a comparative point about the authorial viewpoint and purpose.

Sample response

Dickens describes a bleak scene in a Victorian workhouse. Oliver Twist dares to ask for more food and the employees and the Board are appalled. Trollope describes a very different scene: a picture of excess and a table laden with food. Here there are hams and sirloin, food in abundance, which contrasts with the miserly portions of 'gruel' 'ladled' out to the workhouse inmates. Just as Dickens wants the reader to condemn the meanness of the workhouse, so Trollope wishes to expose inordinate greed.

Trollope's descriptions are very detailed and appropriate for the text's purpose, which is to focus closely on the room and the 'fare' served and to lead up to the final condemnation of such excess. The extract is not directly concerned with the actions of a character. In comparison, Dickens focuses on Oliver's plight, as well as describing the appalling workhouse conditions and indicating his disapproval of such conditions to the reader. Dickens' scene presents a dramatic confrontation whereas the Trollope extract has no character conflict, but it builds to a conclusion where the author's ironic remarks make it clear how he views this greedy archdeacon, who, we are told, regards this excessive food as mere 'ordinary fare'.

There are, however, similarities in style. Trollope emphasises the abundance of food by using lengthy lists (such as the bread details) in long, complex sentences. Dickens also uses a more elaborate style with subordinate clauses in complex sentence structures, especially in the first paragraph when he is describing the workhouse scene. However, his style is more varied. For example, the sentences are shorter in the second paragraph when the emphasis is on movement and action. The short clauses each deal with a separate action, moving the story along at a pace: 'arrived', 'took', 'stationed', 'ranged', 'served', etc.

Practical activity

1 It would be interesting to compare a fictional prose extract with an extract of a different genre, for example to compare Text 31 (the Galsworthy extract) with Text 2 (the poem by U.A. Fanthorpe). Answer this question:

   What different techniques do the writers use to convey the scenes and characters, and how effectively, in your view, do they do this?

   Consider their different purposes, and how the form and structure influence language choices.

2 Compare Text 31 (an extract from *The Man of Property* by Galsworthy) with Text 33 (an extract from *Porterhouse Blue* by Sharpe). In Text 31, Galsworthy depends heavily on crafted speech and the passage needs to be read carefully to pick up on the mood and atmosphere. In Text 33, Sharpe makes far less use of direct speech. What do you think are the differences in authorial intention? How successfully does each bring the meal to life?

3 a Describe a memorable meal or celebration at which you were present. Try to bring the scene to life. Rather than spelling out your feelings, choose your words carefully to give hints to the audience about your attitude to the event. You might like to copy some of the techniques that Galsworthy uses to indicate mood and atmosphere, or take the ironic approach of Dickens or Trollope.

   b Exchange your piece with another student. Assess the techniques you have each used and how successful or unsuccessful you have been in conveying the scene. You could each write a critical commentary on the other's writing, or this could be an oral exercise reading each piece aloud and giving your reactions.

AQA Examiner's tip

1 When writing a comparative essay it helps to use linking words and phrases to join sections together smoothly. They can also signpost a change of direction in your essay (like discourse markers in speech). Here is a simple list:

   a On the one hand

   b On the other hand

   c In contrast with

   d Similarly

   e However

   f Nevertheless

   g In addition to this

   h Also.

   But overuse of such phrases can make writing seem stilted and artificial. So use them carefully.

2 Try to compare both texts simultaneously as you work through your comparative response, not one at a time. For example: 'Just as Dickens wants the reader to condemn the meanness of the workhouse, so Trollope wishes to expose inordinate greed.'

Poetry

Poets and critics throughout the centuries have focused on what we mean by poetry. Here are a few definitions. Which one(s) do you find the most apt?

▦ 'Poetry lifts the veil from the hidden beauty of the world, and makes familiar objects be as if they were not familiar.' (Shelley)

▦ 'Poetry is thoughts that breathe, and words that burn.' (Thomas Gray)

▦ 'Poetry is language in orbit.' (Seamus Heaney)

▦ 'Poetry is when an emotion has found its thought and the thought has found words.' (Robert Frost)

▦ 'Out of the quarrel with others we make rhetoric; out of the quarrel with ourselves we make poetry.' (W.B. Yeats)

▦ 'Poetry is a heightened imagistic use of language that does things to the heart and head.' (Grace Nichols)

You will need to become familiar with *all* of the Anthology poems for your examination. The selection is varied from the poignant Text 4 ('Grandpa's Soup' by Jackie Kay) to the light-hearted prayer for chocolate Text 6 ('Glory Glory Be to Chocolate' by John Agard). Reading and listening to these poems will help you to become more familiar with them. When you study the poems more closely, however, your views of how they should be read may change as you develop your understanding and revise your interpretation of them.

Critical response activity

1 Read each poem aloud. Poetry is meant to be heard, and listening to the words and the **cadences** can be pleasurable in itself. It also helps us to understand the sense.

2 Record different voices reading each poem. Then listen to how altering the **stress** or **intonation** can alter the sense. For example, Text 7 ('Receipt to make Soup' by Alexander Pope) is chant-like, reminiscent of a magic spell, and reading it aloud emphasises the insistent beat. But it can be read at differing paces and with varying stress and intonation. The voice in Text 3 ('The Sweet Menu' by Jeremy Hughes) is entirely different, but its tone could still be varied from a quiet accepting voice to one that sounds more hauntingly lonely, or a mixture of both.

Key terms

Cadence: another word for rhythm.

Stress: emphasis on a syllable or particular word.

Intonation: the way in which the rising, falling and level tones of voice create sound patterns in phrases and sentences.

Link

For more information on tackling the examination questions, see Chapters 9 and 10.

▦ Approaching poetry analysis

As you will remember from Chapter 3 (page 22), the bullet points attached to the examination question are intended to guide your response. The same points can also be used in poetry analysis. This section explains what these bullet points direct you to analyse and it also introduces other useful terms that can be applied to poetry analysis, such as 'tone' and 'mood'. Use this section as a reference source to help you find ways of writing about poems effectively. But remember that each poem is different and applying a checklist approach to analysis can be counterproductive. You risk missing the distinctive power of each poem if you take this approach.

Contexts of production

Knowing the context of production for a poetry text is as important as for any other text. For example, appreciating that James Berry is Jamaican helps us to understand his love for Caribbean produce shown in Text 5. Knowing some details about Jonathan Swift's life and the social and historical context can help us to understand allusions to people like 'King Will' or references to religion and food in the 18th century.

Form

This refers to the genre or type of poem, such as **sonnet**, **elegy**, **haiku**, narrative poem or dramatic monologue, etc. In addition, the form of a poem may be labelled as rhyming, or perhaps as **free verse**. Free verse form uses the varied rhythms of speech to provide its shape. However, poems that use predominantly regular rhyming patterns often also use the rhythms of speech to shape lines. So poems may not easily fit any one category. 'Grandpa's Soup', for example, uses rhyme and repetition of sounds, but its form is not the conventional rhythmical, rhyming poetry (like Pope's). It is free verse, not constrained by regular patterns of **metre**, but shaped by the speaking voice and the points being made.

However, be careful with your usage of the term 'free verse'. It can be a convenient label, but it is more important to focus on the individual poem and how its meaning is created. Recognising the form (and that is not always easy) may be only a starting point that can then shape your expectations and your analysis. Each poem is distinctive and deserves close scrutiny, not just a labelling approach.

Structure

This refers to how a poem is shaped internally, what is the starting point and what details are given to the listener or reader in what order, and with what effect. Just being able to identify the structure is not enough; attempting to assess its impact on the poem's meaning is an important task. It also involves analysing how, and if, **stanzas** (or distinct sections) are used – and with what effect.

'Grandpa's Soup', for example, is not organised in stanzas that are recognisably similar in terms of line length or rhythm. But it definitely has two sections and then a final reflective line that is emphasised by being separated from the main body of the text. There is a break between the first two sections, which suggests that each section is separate and coherent. The poem is structured so that the persona in the first section praises the soup and its ingredients. The poet here makes use of **enjambement** to create a fluid speaking voice. This is when the sense carries on from one line to the next, such as: 'No one makes soup like my Grandpa's / with its diced carrots the perfect size' etc. The second section reiterates how it is 'the best' and links the soup with a reflection on the grandpa's death and how the speaker would miss him after he has gone; how every soup would then be 'sad and wrong after he is gone'.

Of course, there are other ways of looking at how the poem is organised. You could break the sequence down further into smaller units. For example, the author begins with four lines of praise (one section) and then reflects on what the name is for the 'wee soft bits' (a second section). You might decide that there are then several subsections in the second part as well. The final line then reminds us of the first section and the poet's musings about the name for the 'soft wee bits'. It returns the reader full circle back to the initial thoughts of the poem and the perfect soup.

Practical activity

For each poem in the Anthology find out more about the author:

- when they were, or are, writing
- how much they have published
- how their audiences have received them.

Key terms

Sonnet: a traditional poetic form that usually has 14 lines of 10 syllables each, and with a regular rhyming and stress pattern, e.g. Shakespeare's sonnets.

Elegy: a meditative poem of lament, often commemorating someone's death, e.g. Gray's 'Elegy Written in a Country Churchyard'.

Haiku: a word of Japanese origin that means a poem of three lines and a total of 17 syllables (line 1: five syllables, line 2: seven syllables, line 3: five syllables), e.g. William Carlos Williams' 'The Red Wheelbarrow'.

Free verse: a poem that is not constrained by regular metrical patterns, but is shaped by the speaking voice and the points being made.

Metre: from the Greek word 'metron', which means measure. The measurement of a line of poetry, including its length and its number of stresses.

Stanza: group of lines that forms a unit in a poem (often called a verse).

Enjambement: the technique of making the sense of a poem continue from one line to the next, creating a feeling of fluidity.

Research point

Look at an example of a haiku. Then write one of your own. Reflect on the advantages and disadvantages of the form.

■ Critical response activity

Examine the form and structure of Text 3 ('The Sweet Menu'). Write about form in a few sentences and then use a list format to analyse the structure. Remember that there are different ways of unravelling the structure. This activity is essential groundwork when analysing any poem.

After you have completed your work, compare your conclusions with those in the commentary below.

Commentary

Form. This poem uses the 'free verse' form, where the speaker's thoughts shape the arrangement of ideas. It is organised into sections of two lines each, but the line length varies depending upon what is being said. For example, the short line 'a lily' draws attention to the singular flower and echoes the sense of loneliness that pervades the poem. There are much longer lines too such as 'The women who wait the tables spin with trays of drinks and plates'. The speaker here is observing the activity that whirls around him, and the unbroken longer line means that we perceive this activity as something which happens quickly: it 'spins'. The movement is in contrast with the sense of isolation and stillness that surrounds the speaker.

Structure

- ■ The speaker is shown to the table and the surroundings are described: the empty chair opposite, the families, baby and small boy.
- ■ The table decoration: a plastic lily.
- ■ The empty chair opposite is described again.
- ■ The waitresses and activity, and the food eaten.
- ■ Observation about the ceiling and how the light flatters everyone else.
- ■ Eating and drinking and facing the empty chair.
- ■ The waitress approaches, the speaker says he/she would like to talk about the plastic lily.
- ■ The waitress offers the sweet menu and the speaker reflects on how he/she would like to be able to talk about their choices. But the sweet is declined.
- ■ The final activity – a tip is given.
- ■ Reflection on life and this meal: 'it hasn't come to much'.

■ Language

Word choice (or poetic diction)

What kind of lexis does the poet use? Is the use varied? Is the lexis simple, such as the opening line of 'The Sweet Menu' ('I'm shown to a table for two') or more polysyllabic as in 'the descendants of Theobrama Cacao' in 'Glory Glory be to Chocolate'? There are many other ways of describing the choice of lexis, including formal, elaborate, colloquial and **demotic**. A poet can use simple words in simple phrases or sentences and convey a scene or feeling very effectively. For example, 'I eat and drink and face the chair' (Text 3, 'The Sweet Menu') is monosyllabic and there are no adjectives to flesh out the description. It is left to the reader to visualise the scene. But the starkness of it, the bare details, underline the loneliness of the poetic voice. Alternatively a poet can use more elevated lexis such as the description of the pigs in 'The Butcher's Shop' as 'dignified in martyrs' deaths' and juxtapose this with simpler colloquial phrases: 'strung in rows' and 'open-mouthed'. This word choice paints a clear picture of the dead pigs and simultaneously reveals a sympathetic authorial view.

■ Practical activity

Analyse the form and structure of all the other poems along the lines of the analysis of 'The Sweet Menu' in the Critical response activity. You will then be very familiar with the content of each.

■ Key terms

Demotic: everyday, prosaic (ordinary) language.

Critical response activity

Look closely at the word choice in 'The Sweet Menu' and reflect on the type of words and phrases chosen and their effect. You can do this in tabular form as shown below.

Word choice	Reflections
I'm shown	Informal and simple, with the elision of I am. Reader is straight in to the action.
Table for two	Simple collocation. Significant here because speaker is alone.

Carry on with the table, picking out words and phrases that strike you. Then write a few sentences summing up Jeremy Hughes's word choice in this poem and whether you think it is effective or not, bearing in mind what you think the poem is about. Complete this before you read the commentary below.

Commentary

Hughes chooses simple, monosyllabic words such as 'eat', 'drink', 'hot', 'good'. The register is informal and the language is plain. This seems apt to describe a scene that focuses on the loneliness of the speaker, highlighted by repeated reference to the 'other chair' which faces him – empty. Repetition of 'I'd like', 'I eat', 'I tip' emphasises he/she is alone. More dynamic verbs are used to describe the other diners and the staff: the baby is being taught 'to clap'; the waitresses 'spin', 'pirouette' and finally one 'pliés'. There is word play on pliés: it refers to a ballet movement, but she also 'plies' him with the receipt. On the whole, however, the words chosen are simple and the sense is clear.

Figurative language

Figurative language is often referred to as **imagery**. This is language used to bring a scene, idea or object to life. It always involves a comparison, whether obvious (as in a simile) or more concealed as in a metaphor. The resultant phrases cannot be understood literally, for example the butcher's 'meaty smile' or the phrase 'Handfuls hold hidden sunsets'. Judging if imagery is effective can involve asking the question: Does the image illuminate the scene for you and enable you to imagine the character or thing being described? Does it also seem appropriate in the context of the poem?

From your GCSE English you will be familiar with simile, metaphor and **personification**, which are the commonest figures of speech. Each one involves making a comparison, and explanations are given in the table.

Key terms

Imagery: figurative language used to bring a scene, idea or object to life. It usually involves a comparison between two objects or ideas, such as 'The sun is like a red balloon'.

Personification: a type of figurative language when a writer treats an inanimate object or idea as if it were human. For example, 'The wind sighed'.

Simile	A comparison is made obvious by use of 'as' or 'like'. For example, in 'The Butcher's Shop' his fingers are 'fat as sausages'.
Metaphor	This is when the comparison between objects or ideas is not spelled out. For example, the butcher's smile is a 'meaty smile' (Text 1). This is figurative language (not literally true) and the implied comparison is between a piece of meat – the pig's head perhaps – and his smile. It is sinister and effective.
Personification	This is when a poet treats an inanimate object as if it were human. For example, in Text 5 'The Caribbean hills have moved and come'. We know the hills cannot move. Here the poet is in fact using 'hills' to stand for the West Indian produce. Or in Text 6, the cocoa pod 'divine barbaric pod' is spoken of as if it were human and had descendants.

Key terms

Rhythm: the rhythm of a poem refers to the pulse or beat that the listener perceives.

Caesurae: pauses within lines of verse (singular: caesura).

It helps to be aware that whilst imagery is used extensively in poetry, labelling a figure of speech is only the starting point. 'Sun's alphabet drops out of branches' (Text 5) is metaphorical, but it is important to understand the comparison; how does it link with the Caribbean fruits and what is the effect?

Phonological features

These features are referred to as 'sound patterning' in the examination prompts. In poetry, the sounds are particularly important, so you need to be aware of these features and the correct terminology to use:

Feature	Explanation	Example
Rhyme	The commonest kind of rhyming scheme involves the full rhyming of words at the end of lines.	'Veal' and 'steal' (Text 7, lines 1 and 2). The poem is arranged mostly in rhyming couplets so that the listener anticipates the rhyme.
Sound echoes	A poet may play with sounds for effect.	'Brownies candies cookies' (Text 6, line 9). The second syllable of each word is echoed and the sibilants ('s' sounds) are repeated. There is a sense of abundance here (the 's' marks the plural).
Onomatopoeia	This refers to words that sound like their meaning or whose sound echoes their sense.	'Smooth' (Text 5, line 27) with its long vowels suggests an even texture; or 'clogs' (Text 1, line 11) with its short vowel and harsh consonant seems apt to describe something (in this case sawdust) that sticks to a surface.
Alliteration	Sound patterning in which the writer repeats the initial sounds of adjacent words.	'Paper parcel' (Text 1, line 14) or 'Posters of pop stars' (Text 5, line 38). Notice also the clever play on sounds in this phrase: the 's' sounds repeated and the sound echoes in the second syllable: 'steers and stars'.
Rhythm	The rhythm of a poem refers to the pulse or beat that the listener perceives. Much traditional poetry (the Alexander Pope poem for example) has a clear rhythmical framework.	There are between five and seven syllables in each line in Text 6 but each line has two strong stresses. The short lines and the insistent beat create a chant-like feel, reminiscent of a simple nursery rhyme.
		Rhythm in the other poems is less easy to discern and is more variable from line to line. For example, the opening of Text 5 begins with a line that is a bit of a tongue twister and where each word is given equal, slow emphasis. Compare this with a later line: 'Red buses pass for donkeys now' with its simple syntax and easy rhythm: four beats to the line.
		Poets often use pauses (**caesurae**), which alter a poem's rhythm and the impact of what is being said. For example, look at the dramatic pause (caused by a full stop) in line 13 of Text 1, before 'All the way home'.

Link

For more information about rhythm and metre see Chapter 7, page 51.

Think about it

Remember the poet T.S. Eliot's statement: 'Genuine poetry can communicate before it is understood', and do not get irritated if you cannot unravel the sense of every phrase immediately. Enjoy the sounds and images.

Grammar

In a poem you will be concerned with syntax (word order) and how this affects meaning and the prominence given to particular words and phrases. You will also need to be aware of contrasting uses of simple, compound and complex sentence constructions.

Compare, for example, the syntax of 'there is water in the bottle but the flower is plastic' (a compound sentence that gives details clearly and sequentially) with the elliptical opening to Text 5: 'Handfuls hold hidden sunset / stuffing up bags / and filling up the London baskets'. Handfuls of what? Whose hands? It is intriguing.

Mood

The mood of a poem, or its atmosphere, is created by the poet's choice of form, language and structure. So the mood of Text 4 ('Grandpa's Soup') could be said to be celebratory (praise for the soup) but with some poignant sad musings in the second half.

Tone

The tone usually refers more specifically to the tone of voice of the writer. The tone could be sarcastic, jaunty, light-hearted, sombre, melancholic, etc., or varied from one section to another. The writer's tone and the mood created are often similar. Here, Jackie Kay's tone is a mixture of happy and sad, joy at her reflections and then melancholy at the thought of a future without her grandpa. The mood created by the whole poem is similar: the reader feels this mixture of happiness and sadness.

Overall meaning

The overall meaning of a poem that is conveyed to the reader and/or the listener is a combination of all of these choices of form, structure and language and the mood that is evoked. Your reaction to a poem and your judgement of it is a very individual activity. We would all agree that Text 5 describes Caribbean fruit and vegetables, and you would certainly be misreading it if you did not grasp that the poet is describing Caribbean produce in London markets. There will also be some consensus about the narrative here. But, which images appeal to our imagination and why will vary, as will our associations with particular phrases. The art in poetry criticism is being able to explain why perhaps a line like 'mango soaked in sunrise' strikes you and why it works in the structure of the poem. It could be said that the use of the word 'soaked' is appropriate and evocative because it implies that the fruit has been bathed in sunshine and is fully ripe and brightly coloured. The mango brings some of the Caribbean warmth with it to London. It is one of several fruits that the writer depicts, and the overall effect is to add to the sense of colourful abundance.

Text 2: 'Eating Out'

Ursula Fanthorpe captures the humour, embarrassment and poignancy of remembering what it was like to eat out with her family. The narrative of the poem takes us from early adventures in eating with all the stuffiness of manners having to be learned, to more adventurous eating out and reflections on her parents' approaches. She also reveals subtly what she felt about her parents and their relationship.

Practical activity

Writing your own poem can really help you to appreciate how a poem is formed, the choices an author has to make about lexis and structure, and how to shape the meanings.

1 Choose one of the following tasks:

   a Write a short poem about a particular food you like or loathe.

   b Write a pastiche of one of the poems in the Anthology. (See Chapter 5, page 32 for an explanation of 'pastiche'.)

2 Read the poem aloud and give an oral commentary to an audience, explaining your choices and any difficulties you encountered.

Critical response activity

Answer the question:

What does Fanthorpe have to say in Text 2 about eating out and how effectively does she convey her thoughts and memories?

Here are a few prompts to help you analyse the poem and to write a coherent answer. Make notes and then write your answer in full before reading the sample answer overleaf.

Language: work through the poem chronologically, unravelling the sense and noting phrases or words that strike you. Think about why the poet chooses the words she does, how she varies the lexis and the grammar. Also, does she make any use of figurative language and phonological features, and with what effect? (Do not strain to find examples. If there is no figurative language that strikes you, then leave this out.)

Form and structure: reflect on the form the poem takes and then analyse the structure:

■ what is being said stanza by stanza

■ how points are linked

■ the effects achieved by the use of enjambement and caesurae.

Tone and mood: think about:

■ when and how the tone and mood of the poem changes and the impact that has on the reader

■ why she ends with a single line and how this would be said.

Overall meaning:

■ finally, assess your view of the poem including where your sympathies lie, as well as how effectively the scenes, characters and sentiments are brought to life.

Sample response

Notice the close focus on word choice, together with some comment and explanation.

Fanthorpe emphasises the formality and the stuffiness of her first 'adventures' into eating out. The events sound like an ordeal and she finds having to behave well 'indigestible'. Using a word from the semantic field of food is entirely appropriate here to stress her reaction to the outings. There is a sense of artificiality conveyed by the verbs 'rehearsed', 'supervised', 'explained'. They may have been 'adventures' with the excitement of the 'unknown', but she had to behave well and in a prescribed, correct way. The image of the napkin conscientiously tucked in stresses that her parents are following convention whilst the grammatically truncated sentences with the elliptical 'Choice of cutlery supervised' sound cold and impersonal. Human agency is removed, the reader is not told who explains or who supervises, even though we assume that it is the poet's father.

An exact grammatical point made and the resultant mood explored.

However, Fanthorpe's tone changes in stanza three when 'Mother' is named, and the caring approach of taking her outside to recover is mentioned. The poet then moves to what sound like real adventures, her father introducing her to more exotic foods. The lexis changes and the simpler, more colloquial 'handle' and 'pocket' are used, rather than the earlier more elaborate words. However, the lobster is addressed as 'ritual consumption', perhaps suggesting some distaste rather than any pleasure or relish in the dish.

The point about there being no elaborate imagery is followed by a comment which shows that a simple detail (not figurative) can still be evocative.

The last two stanzas are very touching. Fanthorpe chooses simple lexis and refers to 'my last outing with him'. She is not heavily descriptive, there is no elaborate imagery, but the detail of 'teacakes in a Petworth teashop' is sufficient to conjure up a picture for the reader. The most poignant line in the poem is the understated 'He leaned heavy on my arm'. The reader might expect the grammatically correct 'heavily' (an adverb qualifying the verb 'leaned') but 'heavy' is much more effective. We sense his dead weight, and remember we have been told this was the last outing. Despite this sense of frailty, her father summons enough strength to play his usual role of taking charge and ordering.

Look at how the poignant line is really explored.

Some close attention is paid to sounds/phonological features.

The caesura after 'ordering' is touching and the reader is left to imagine his death. The phrase 'Mother died older, later' is memorable because of the repeated assonance of 'er' sounds. Fanthorpe's writing is very economical; no words are wasted. We are left finally with the interesting contradiction that her mother was both autocratic and subservient. That she played the role of allowing the father to be in charge is emphasised in the last italicised line.

Comment made on the effect of the poet's choices. Features are not just identified.

A final, brief evaluation of the poem is given.

This poem has a staccato (abrupt) feel to it in the first few stanzas, with many end-stopped lines, but then there is more fluency. Fanthorpe uses some enjambement in the second half of the poem when she is more expansive about her father's advice. For example, she is told 'not / To eat all the petit fours' and 'he initiated me / Into the ritual consumption of lobster'. The use of pauses in the poem and the mixture of abrupt phrases and more fluid ones effectively mimics the variety of a speaking voice.

This poetry criticism tackles the poem chronologically, commenting on features as the writer works through the analysis. With a short poem this is the most straightforward way of approaching the task. The last paragraph makes a final evaluation about how evocative the poem is.

'Eating Out' is concise and economically worded. The writer's memories are clearly evoked and her attitudes to her parents are revealed in a moving and reflective poem.

Remember this is only one interpretation of the poem. Poetry is often ambiguous and this is part of its attraction. The interpretation of a phrase and the associations it evokes in different readers can vary greatly.

Text 6: 'Glory Glory be to Chocolate'

This is a poem of praise, a light-hearted, clever acknowledgement of the delights of chocolate. The quotation from Debrah Waterhouse's book *Why Women Need Chocolate* links chocolate cravings with women, but calls such desires 'Eve's blessing'. This use of religious language emphasises that the poem takes the form of a prayer. John Agard uses this idea as his starting point.

The contexts of production for this text are important. Understanding the author's use of a biblical form and appreciating the allusions and references will help to shape your response to the poem. Look at the background information and then do the Critical response activity.

Background information

- Refer to page 4 in the Anthology for essential background information on John Agard.
- The phrase 'Naughty but Nice' has interesting, disputed origins. In lines two and three, Agard is referring to Salman Rushdie who wrote *The Satanic Verses*. He supposedly coined the phrase when he was working in advertising in the 1980s. The slogan was used to advertise cream cakes. However, this was not its first appearance. A comic music hall song of 1873 by Arthur Lloyd had the same title. That was possibly its first use.
- Doxology is a formula of praise to God and this poem could be said to adopt this form, investing chocolate with god-like properties. 'Glory be' is a recognisable phrase used in religious worship, but Agard adapts it and makes it more hyperbolic, yet childlike and flippant in tone with the repetition of 'Glory'.
- *Theobroma cacao* is the full name for the cacao or cocoa tree.

Commentary

1   The humorous quotation from Debrah Waterhouse gives the writing an air of authority. It reinforces John Agard's point about the value of chocolate and sets the tone of the whole piece.

2   References in academic texts are acknowledged by notes in brackets, so this reinforces the apparent seriousness of this piece.

3   'So' is an informal discourse marker, used emphatically in Text 6. Agard is communicating with his readers and letting them know with absolute certainty that chocolate is worth praising.

4   'Manifestations' is a word of Latin origin with biblical resonance. Here it means chocolate of all types and varieties.

5   Figurative language is very striking. 'Ringing the bells of our taste buds' suggests a food that we cannot ignore, one that overpowers us, stimulates us and makes us alert. The image of imps is effective as they are wild, uncontrollable demons, which links back to the biblical overtones and the sense that eating chocolate is sinful (naughty) but nice. Here the 'Cinnamon-flavoured little imps' 'twinkle at the tongue', hinting at the exciting flashes of flavour that hit our taste buds.

6   Chocolate is seen as a wonderful contributor to happiness. It releases endorphins that lift the mood. But here Agard calls them appropriately endomorphins (an endomorph is a person with a high proportion of fat tissue). We are reminded of how fattening chocolate is! He then questions how anyone could criticise the eating of chocolate as sinful. The oxymoron of 'divine barbaric pod' is amusing and this final speech is addressed directly to cocoa pods.

Critical response activity

Answer the following questions. They will direct you to think about the form of the poem and its structure, as well as to consider some word choices, the internal structure, the use of figurative language and the overall meaning conveyed.

1   What effect does the use of the Waterhouse quotation have on your response to the poem?

2   Why does Agard put the second and third lines in brackets?

3   Why does he declare, 'So, I say it twice?'

4   What is meant by 'in all its manifestations'?

5   How effectively does he describe the types of chocolate? Look particularly at the figurative phrases, 'ring the tastebud bells' and 'Cinnamon-flavoured little imps / that twinkle at the tongue.'

6   Explain the sense of the last six lines and comment on any striking phrases.

7   Apart from 'glory glory be' what other elements in the poem are modelled on a prayer?

8   Looking at the structure, what effect does the line arrangement have on the reader?

7   Notice the continuation of lexis in the semantic field of religion: 'blessing', 'glory', 'sin', 'divine god'. He ends on a rhetorical question: how could anyone be so critical when eating chocolate makes everyone a god? (An extreme note to finish on.)

8   The first two bracketed lines are balanced by the two penultimate lines. All other stanzas have three lines. The first three stanzas praise chocolate, the next two stanzas give us some manifestations, and then the section that begins with the exclamation 'O' changes tack and asserts that no one can argue about its divine qualities. The final line is set apart to emphasise the effect of eating chocolate – often called 'the food of the gods'.

Comparing poems with other types of texts

Critical response activity

1   Once you are familiar with each poem, complete a critical analysis of each one along the lines of our close scrutiny of Texts 2 and 6 looking at:

a   form

b   structure

c   language: lexical (word) choice, figurative language and phonological features/sound patterning

d   tone

e   mood

f   overall meaning.

2   Now think about the topics and themes that each poem deals with. Try sorting the poems according to food themes and topics (some suggestions have been provided in the table). You could copy out the table and then continue, looking at possible texts to compare with each poem.

Poem	Food topics/ themes	Other possible texts for comparison
'The Butcher's shop'	Contrast between the reality of the bloody butcher's shop and the romantic image of animals: snowy sheep.	Text 9: the *Mail Online*, Text 11: Vegetarian Society, Text 15: Hygiene Improvement Regulations.
'Eating out'	Eating out in cafés and restaurants. Parental attitudes.	Text 31: Galsworthy extract, Text 12: restaurant reviews, Text 19: the transcript, Text 26: Hoggart's article about food in the 1920s and 1930s, Text 18: transcript of a family meal.
'Glory Glory Be to Chocolate'	The delights of chocolate, the pleasure of food.	Text 17: Nigella's monologue, Text 29: Trollope, Text 33: the feast in *Porterhouse Blue*.

Critical response activity

Choose one of the following three questions and write a comparative essay. Use a poem as one of your texts (but compare it with a different form of text). Remember the advice given in Chapter 5 on page 36 – you should aim to consider aspects of the two texts side by side rather than dealing with the whole of one text and then another.

1   Compare two texts from the Anthology that focus on the pleasures of eating. In your answer write about some of the following where appropriate:

■   contexts of production and reception

■   form and structure

■   figurative language

■   sound patterning.

■   word choice

■   grammar

■   layout and presentation.

2   Compare two texts that focus on families and food. In your answer write about some of the points listed under Question 1 above where appropriate.

3   Compare two texts that highlight different attitudes to what we should and should not eat. In your answer write about some of the points listed under Question 1 above where appropriate.

Commentary

It is essential to choose your texts carefully. Identify the texts that clearly focus on the points in the question. 'Eating out' or 'Grandpa's Soup' would be suitable poems to use when answering question 2. Either one could be compared with Text 18 (the transcript of a family meal) or Text 26 (which talks about the food that families ate in the 1920s and 1930s).

Plan your answer carefully, making use of the prompts where they are helpful. You do not have to tackle them in the order they are given in the examination paper. Choose an essay framework that seems appropriate. If you compare 'Eating out' with the transcript, your essay framework may look like this:

- Form: emphasise the difference in purpose and audience for each form. The transcript has an internal audience of the family, as well as the audience of those studying spoken language. The form of the poem is couplets, but not rhyming and the audience would be readers or listeners, a wide audience.

- Contexts: the context of the meal table is a private one with only the family involved. In the poem the contexts change from early 'adventures' in eating, to London cuisine and then finally to the Petworth teashop. The poem's purpose is very different from the purpose of the family interaction. However, there are similarities in that the poem reveals the nature of some family relationships, as does the transcript.

- Structure: compare the order of action in the transcript with the way the poet orders the poem. Obviously the different purposes will influence the structure. An informal, spontaneous family meal appears to have a random structure with many topic changes. The poem is a much more structured text with no words wasted.

- Language (including word choice, figurative, language sound patterning). Note that this will probably be your longest section. You would compare the informality of the exchanges in the transcript with the mixed register of the poem (both elaborate and informal). Link these comments with purpose and also reflect on the effects of particular phrases. For example, what is revealed about the relationship between Mother and the family members by the mother's comments such as 'Well, here we are' (Text 18, line 21)? Compare this with the mother's language and behaviour in Text 2, for example her declarative statement: 'I'll have whatever you're having, dear.' Have confidence in your own selection of phrases and your judgements of their effects.

- Mood and tone and overall meaning.

Having worked your way through a comparison of the two texts, try to sum up the overall impact of each. What tone do the speakers take in the transcript? Does it vary and why? Similarly, does the poet vary the mood and tone of the poem and for what purpose? Finally, sum up what is revealed about family relationships in each text.

AQA Examiner's tip

When analysing poems:

- Read each poem aloud several times.

- Use the examination prompts (such as word choice) to provide a framework for your response.

- Do not expect all of the prompts to be of equal significance in your discussions of a poem. Do not force your analysis to fit the prompts. They are there to guide your thinking.

- Each poem is distinctive. Approach a poem with an open mind and not a formulaic approach.

Link

For more information on planning your essay see Chapters 2, 3 and 9.

7 Drama

This chapter covers:

- an introduction to the crafted language of drama

- sharpening and developing skills of analysis

- close analysis of two texts from the Anthology

- comparing drama with another literary form.

Research point

In 2011, the BBC advertised a new drama serial, *The Crimson Petal and the White*, as 'A tale of love, lust, desire and revenge'. Such a description could be applied to many plays and films both now and in the past. The themes are of universal interest and, of course, the statement could be used to advertise *Titus Andronicus*, with special emphasis on revenge.

It would be interesting to find further examples of plays or films that focus on these themes. Search the internet, newspapers and magazines and you will see how popular such themes are. Look particularly for mention of 'revenge'.

Key terms

Revenge tragedy: a play where one or more characters are spurred on by the desire to avenge perceived wrongs that have been committed against them. Their vengeance usually involves much bloodshed.

Research point

Find out more about the genre and history of revenge tragedy.

The essence of drama is contrast and conflict, between characters, scenes and ideas. The two excerpts from the Anthology that we shall examine contrast greatly with each other, but *within* each extract there is contrast and conflict too. *Titus Andronicus* is a Shakespearian tragedy and *The Importance of Being Earnest* is a light-hearted comedy of manners.

Text 21: *Titus Andronicus*

This is one of Shakespeare's earliest plays, first performed in about 1590 when Elizabeth I was on the throne. It is set in the late days of the Roman Empire but the events are fictitious. Shakespeare probably drew on a story originally by Seneca (a Roman playwright) and he used some ideas from Ovid's *Metamorphoses* (a collection of stories written in poetic form). *Titus Andronicus* is a grim, bloody story with the flawed hero Titus at its heart. The play's plot is complex and it pivots around a number of feuds and rivalries, but revenge is the driving force. Everyone appears to be after vengeance for what they perceive to be wrongs done to them. The play is very much in the tradition of Elizabethan and Jacobean **revenge tragedy**, 'a welter of bloody mayhem and revenge' (Jay Wright, director of a 2008 production of the play).

Background information

The characteristics of revenge tragedy

- Characters seeking vengeance are often spurred on by the acts of others, which they judge to have been dishonourable (killing of a brother, a king, etc.). The biblical idea of 'an eye for an eye' is then followed.

- The plays are usually set in a corrupt state where justice is unlikely to be carried out thereby forcing individuals to take revenge into their own hands.

- The revenge crimes often surpass in horror (and quantity) the original crimes.

- Madness, feigned or real, is a common theme, as are ranting and long rhetorical speeches that build to big climaxes.

- Moral questions are raised.

- The ending often involves a high body count culminating in the avenger and the avenged dying in a bloody finale.

- Law and order and state power are usually re-established after the final killings.

In 1590 Thomas Kyd's *Spanish Tragedy*, one of the earliest in the genre, was extremely popular. Later dramatists included Webster with *The Duchess of Malfi* and *The White Devil*. Shakespeare adapted and developed the genre in *Hamlet*, which is a much more psychologically complex play, with more focus on introspection than the usual revenge tragedies.

Background information

Titus Andronicus

Context of production and reception:

- The Elizabethan era was one where public executions, bear-baiting and cockfighting were commonplace. So an Elizabethan audience for this play would probably have been less appalled than an audience today by events like the cutting off of hands. However, the play would still have shocked, with its multiple grotesque horrors such as the baking of the heads in a pie. However, the play was very popular – a testament to the fascination with horror, compelling and repulsive at the same time.

Context for the scene in Text 21:

- Earlier in the play, Titus has slain his own son. Later, two of his other sons are murdered and his daughter Lavinia is raped and mutilated by the sons of Tamora (Queen of the Goths and wife of Saturninus the Emperor). This all sparks off a cycle of revenge. Immediately before the extract from Act V scene II, Tamora appears dressed up as a character called Revenge and her sons appear as Rape and Murder. She tries to trick Titus by saying these masqueraders will find and kill Chiron and Demetrius (the real names of her sons) and that they will avenge the wrongs done. Titus recognises the sons and after Tamora has left he exacts his punishment as portrayed in the scene.
- After the killing of Titus and Saturninus, order is restored and Lucius becomes the next Emperor.

The dramatic extract: A brief overview of the action

Titus has the longest turns and dominates the stage in Scene II. He reveals that he is not mad and that he has recognised Tamara's sons who were guilty of Lavinia's rape. His vengeance is speedy; their throats are cut and Lavinia ''tween her stumps doth hold / The basin that receives your guilty blood' (lines 34 and 35).

In Scene III there is more interaction, with dialogue between Saturninus and Titus and some shorter, more rapid exchanges before the killing of Lavinia. The final revelation, with its grim black humour, is appalling: 'the mother daintily hath fed' on the pie containing the heads of her sons. The catalogue of horror ends with three killings and a stage strewn with bodies.

Form and structure

The form here is clearly a play genre that employs **blank verse**. The structure of the scenes is concerned with the order of events and their dramatic impact. Scene III begins with a tense exchange between Lucius and the Emperor, followed by Marcus trying to reduce the tension, asking them to 'break the parle' and requesting that their quarrels should be 'quietly debated'. Then Titus enters and there is a flurry of apparently pleasant welcomes followed by Titus recounting a story about a father slaying his daughter. Tension is increased as the audience are initially unsure why this story is being narrated. Titus extracts agreement from the Emperor that this slaying in the story was 'well done'. This is quickly followed by 'Die, Die, Lavinia' and the shocking killing of his own daughter. The pace of action speeds up. The audience know what is about to be revealed (this is called **dramatic irony**) but are kept in suspense waiting for the gruesome explanation about the contents of the pie. The revelation is followed by three murders.

The overall structure of the scenes, the sequence of events, is crafted to create tension and to surprise the audience. The structure of individual speeches is carefully created. Look, for example, at Titus's long speech of 40 lines in Scene II (lines 17–57) beginning with 'Come, come, Lavinia'.

■ Critical response activity

Using a table similar to the one shown here, examine the structure of Titus's speech (lines 17–57). Focus on the content, on what he says and in what order, and then make comments on the dramatic impact of different phrases and sections.

The first section of the speech has been summed up in the left-hand column and the right-hand column contains comments. Continue adding sections to the table before you look at the commentary below.

Sections of the speech	Initial thoughts on the dramatic impact
Initial address to Lavinia and others, telling everyone that they are now 'bound' and must listen to his speech.	Titus brandishing a knife is threatening and the long explanation creates tension as the audience waits for some action.

Commentary

Here is a table that sums up the stages in the speech. Analysing it in this way will help you to appreciate how Shakespeare builds tension and leads the audience slowly to the moment when Titus cuts the throats of Tamora's two sons. In your answer you will need to break down the sections further by looking closely at the word choice, grammar, etc.

Sections of the speech	Initial thoughts on the dramatic impact
Initial address to Lavinia and others, telling everyone that they are now 'bound' and must listen to his speech.	Titus brandishing a knife is threatening and the long explanation creates tension as the audience waits for some action.
Lines 20–31: Direct address to the 'villains', 'the inhuman traitors' – a résumé of their appalling offences.	Evokes sympathy for Lavinia and Titus.
Lines 32–47: Titus tells them exactly what he will do: bake the pasty and make the 'strumpet' mother eat it.	Horrific details, audience on edge of seats: Titus says he will 'grind your bones to dust'.
Lines 48–55: More explaining about what he will do, culminating in the throat cutting itself.	More ghastly details, reinforcing the horror of the scene and adding to the audience tension. Spectacle of killing on stage – very dramatic.
Final two lines: Titus announces he will go off and be the cook.	Anticlimactic, but rather grotesque detail. He is personally going to supervise this cookery and give the pie to the mother.

Critical response activity

Now look at Scene III and analyse the whole scene in a similar way to your analysis of Titus's speech, working out the structure of the scene and reflecting on the dramatic impact of different sections. This should help you to understand how Shakespeare crafts the scene and it is useful groundwork for the language analysis that we will be looking at in the next section.

The crafted language of drama

Shakespeare's intention is to create characters that are convincing to the audience, characters that we want to listen to and watch, and action that keeps us engrossed. In this scene the characters use a mixture of figurative language, down-to-earth lexis and grander phrases and allusions (references to other texts). For example, the analogy of Lavinia with 'spring' (line 21) or Saturninus's figurative use of 'sun' to refer to his own position of power contrast with simple everyday phrases such as 'Why, there they are'.

More elaborate phrases include lines 90–93 when Titus uses tripling (the power of three) to enforce his point that Virginius's murder was justified: 'A reason mighty, strong, and effectual / A pattern, president, and lively warrant / For me, most wretched, to perform the like.' Throughout both scenes there are allusions to classical authors such as Ovid and Livy (about Virginius). The variety keeps us interested and there are features that replicate the features of talk, such as repetition of a colloquial phrase like 'Come, come'. However, you will have noticed that the form chosen is blank verse, a poetic style that Shakespeare uses in his plays. He also uses prose, but the scenes we have here, scenes between the high-ranking Romans, and scenes of high drama, are usually expressed in blank verse.

Blank verse is unrhymed. Shakespeare uses a metre (this refers to the rhythmical pattern of beats in the line) called **iambic pentameter**. Pentameter refers to the number of 'iambic feet' in the line. An iambic foot consists of an **unstressed syllable** followed by a **stressed syllable**, shown as u and / respectively. Five iambic feet make up a regular line, which has 10 **syllables**. This is the framework that Shakespeare uses and adapts. However, he does vary the line length and stress pattern to avoid a tedious unvarying metre.

Here are two lines of regular length (lines 34–35), showing the pattern of stressed and unstressed syllables.

```
u   /   u   /   u  /  u  /   u       /
```
His one hand yet is left to cut your throats,

```
u     /   u  /   u   /   u    /    u   /
```
Whiles that La-vin-ia 'tween her stumps doth hold

This is the basic underlying pattern, but in performance actors will often deviate from the regular pattern of stress and intonation to achieve particular emphasis and to reflect natural speech rhythms. Also, you will see that Shakespeare varies the line length and the rhythm at times for different effects. Look, for example, at the quick-fire interaction (lines 86 and 87) between Titus and Saturninus. The shortened lines create the pace.

So the blank verse system is a framework that Shakespeare can adapt to achieve dramatic variety.

Lexis and figurative language, grammar and sound patterning

You are familiar with the terms 'lexis', 'figurative language', 'grammar' and 'sound patterns' from previous chapters. These terms are all interlinked; the words we choose and how we arrange them, the sounds we stress and the comparisons we make all contribute to the meaning. For example, look at the following line from Titus's long speech in Scene II:

> Here stands the spring whom you have stain'd with mud,

> This goodly summer with your winter mix'd;

Titus uses figurative language, for example Lavinia is being compared with the spring, with all its freshness and new hope. Tamara's sons have 'stain'd' this spring 'with mud'. We usually associate a spring with fresh water, but here Titus creates the image of water that has been clogged and spoiled with dirt. The lexis is simple and monosyllabic, and the rhythm clear and emphatic.

He adds a further analogy: Lavinia represents summer in all its brightness, but this has now become 'mix'd' with the cold of winter, associated with death. This is a simple but effective description. Look at the syntax too and the use of antithesis in the second line to emphasise the contrast. There are sound patterns in the lines as well: the repetition of soft sibilants ('s' sounds) in the alliterative 'stands', 'spring', 'stain'd' and then 'summer'. 'Mud' and 'mix'd' both end with the same harsh consonant in contrast with the sounds associated with the gentle Lavinia.

Key terms

Iambic: an iambic foot consists of an unstressed syllable followed by a stressed syllable, shown as u and / respectively. Five iambic feet make up a regular line, which has 10 syllables.

Pentameter: (from the Latin for 'five') refers to the number of iambic feet in the line.

Unstressed syllable: a unit of pronunciation that is not emphasised (this is shown as 'u').

Stressed syllable: a unit of pronunciation that is emphasised (this is shown as an oblique stroke, '/').

Syllable: a unit of pronunciation where there is one vowel sound. Monosyllabic words have one syllable: 'I', 'cat', 'me'. Polysyllabic words have several syllables: re-venge, wel-come, en-ter-tain.

Research point

There are many classical allusions in the text. Find out about the references to Philomel and Progne (Procne) and Virginius. Think about why Titus uses such references.

Critical response activity

1 Take the whole of Titus's long speech (lines 17–57) and write an analysis of the language. You should comment on:

    a form and structure (look at how the blank verse is used and be aware of the sequence of points in the speech)

    b the dramatic language (lexis and figurative language, grammar and sound patterning, where relevant).

    Write your account in coherent prose, rather than notes. You can work your way through the speech chronologically focusing on what strikes you as significant.

2 You could also take the whole of Scene III and examine the language closely. In this case, just make notes about striking features.

Commentary

Here is an example of how you might begin your answer to Question 1:

Titus begins his speech with an appeal to Lavinia and everyone present to look at how 'thy foes are bound'. He uses the colloquial 'stop their mouths' to bluntly tell Publius and his helpers to gag Chiron and Demetrius, and he warns everyone that what will follow are 'fearful words'. He then addresses the characters with an exclamation 'O villains', a blunt form of address that characterises them immediately. Later they are referred to as 'wretches' and 'inhuman traitors', and he also repeats 'villains' for emphasis.

Titus then turns to his daughter Lavinia and addresses her as 'the spring' and 'goodly summer'.

Refer to the work done earlier in the chapter on lines 21 and 22 to help you in composing your analysis of these lines. Then continue with your close scrutiny of the language.

Practical activity

1 Make a list of all the words in the extract that we would be unlikely to use now. Use an etymological dictionary to find out what their sense would have been in Shakespeare's time. You could start the list with: 'Fie', 'Oft' and 'bind them sure'.

2 Find out what the word 'pastie' signified to an Elizabethan audience (in addition to a kind of pie).

Talk features

Using features of natural speech can help to bring characters to life. Otherwise dialogue and speeches can sound like formal textbook extracts rather than real spoken language. Obviously lexis, idiomatic expressions, slang and ways of addressing people change. Few of us now say 'Fie' for example (line 4, Scene II), and 'boots' as a verb today refers to booting up a computer or hitting something. Here (line 63, Scene III) the sense is 'What use or what advantage' (where 'boot' comes from the Old English 'bot' meaning 'advantage'). It is important to understand that semantic change can sometimes make it difficult to be certain of the sense.

Shakespeare animates his characters and makes them speak convincingly, with a mixture of rhetoric (look at the rhetorical questions, for example in Scene II, line 85) and more down-to-earth lexis and sentence constructions. Titus uses elision ('Will't') and ellipsis ('Not I') and repetition, as we all do in real speech.

Dramatic action

We have been examining aspects of the language, but it is important to remember that drama is action taking place over time and there is more to see and listen to than just the words. The body language, the paralinguistics and, of course, the action and the spectacle all contribute to the dramatic impact and the meaning. Drama is a fascinating genre and plays are reinterpreted anew in every production.

In this extract there are several gruesome killings. There is also the spectre of a mutilated Lavinia on stage, and finally her violent death. There is contrast in the language and between the characters and their ways of speaking, from expressive descriptions to imperative utterances like 'Die, die'. There is clearly conflict that culminates in cold-blooded decapitations and in rasher, more explosive and unexpected violence. It is a disturbing and visceral finale. So, what sense do we make of it all? The avengers and the avenged come to the same end. Critics are divided about how to rate this early tragedy, as it undoubtedly lacks the striking poetry of an *Othello* or *Hamlet*. However, moral questions are raised about vengeance, about corrupt states, about honour. Theatrically the play and a climactic scene like this succeed because they offer the audience variety, conflict and plenty of spectacle, with many twists and turns and surprises.

Connecting *Titus Andronicus* with the food theme of the Anthology may not be immediately obvious – cannibalism of the worst kind, a mother eats her sons. Food is supposed to nourish and be associated with sensual pleasure and communal activities. Here it is a weapon of a most extreme revenge.

Text 20: *The Importance of Being Earnest* by Oscar Wilde

Oscar Wilde was born in Dublin in 1854 and is probably better known for his wit and his lifestyle than for some of his plays. Witticisms from this play include the well-known quotation: 'The truth is rarely pure and never simple'.

The Importance of Being Earnest was first performed in 1895 and was a huge success in the West End. It is a comedy that pokes fun at the etiquette and values of Victorian society: the apparent reverence for duty and hard work, the importance of honour and reputation and the acceptance of a rigid class system. But above all it satirises the hypocrisy of those who purport to be paragons of virtue. Furthermore, it does it with humour, through such irreverent characters as Jack (whose alternative identity is Ernest) and Algernon, and the two women in this extract.

Background information

- You can find out more about Wilde's life and his works from websites such as www.sparknotes.com/lit/earnest as well as the full text of the play, some critical comments about it and a synopsis of the action.

- The context for this scene is that in order to escape the country and go up to town (London), Jack has pretended that he has a brother Ernest whom he visits there. In reality Jack uses the name Ernest when he is in town, and under this name he has just become engaged to Gwendolen. She decides to make a surprise visit to him at his country house where Cecily lives under Jack's guardianship. Cecily – a romantic dreamer – has been enamoured with the idea of this brother Ernest, but has never, of course, met him until Jack's dandyish friend Algernon arrives prior to this scene and pretends he is Ernest. Cecily rapidly falls for him and before the scene in the Anthology, he proposes to her. So, at the point of the extract both women believe mistakenly that the Ernest they know is one and the same character and they are therefore rivals in love.

Practical activity

This is a wonderful scene to act out properly, with its pregnant pauses, its polite exchanges and its undercurrents of hatred. Each character is trying to outdo the other. There is tension, and the tea ceremony with all its polite etiquette is the centre of the scene. It builds from restrained criticism and veiled insults to the open outbursts at the end.

Cast the scene, read it through and then enact it, taking on board Wilde's stage directions. Note how these stage directions are more detailed compared with the limited ones provided by Shakespeare in *Titus Andronicus*.

■ Critical response activity

Write an answer to the question:

How does Wilde make this scene dramatically interesting?

Here are some prompts to help in the analysis:

1 What do you understand by the term 'dramatically interesting'?

2 What impressions do you have of each character from the initial exchanges about walks and the countryside?

3 What is amusing about the behaviour of Cecily and Gwendolen and their actions and reactions in lines 23–34?

4 What is dramatic about the final outbursts (line 35 to the end)?

5 Looking back at the exchange, what features does Wilde use to try to replicate real talk?

Commentary

1 A scene that is dramatically interesting can contain revelations of character or clashes between them. Text 20 contains many examples of this; there is often tension between characters and the audience are kept in suspense for long periods. Exchanges of barbed insults can be dramatically interesting: who is going to win in this encounter? Also, the situation, with the restraining influence of the servants, makes for humour, because the characters are keeping up a façade of politeness. The hatred is palpable but the convention of polite conversation is amusingly adhered to.

2 In the initial exchanges Gwendolen sets the agenda with a direct question. Cecily's reply is relatively polite, but Gwendolen takes the amusingly perverse view that she would not like the crowds, whereas the picture the audience imagines is of open countryside. Cecily's tone is supposedly sweet, but her interrogative retort is cuttingly critical. Each character seems equally strong, although the younger Cecily appears more nervous and less used to such exchanges. Gwendolen then shifts the topic and offers faint praise by qualifying 'a well-kept garden' with the adverb 'quite'. Cecily is aware of the veiled criticism and her effusive polite 'So glad you like it' is probably expressed sarcastically.

Gwendolen declares, disingenuously, that she had no idea there were flowers in the country, but Cecily's rejoinder is clever. She is not to be outdone. She links common flowers with the notion of Gwendolen being common. Gwendolen now assumes the role of the cosmopolitan Londoner and becomes blunter and declares that the country is boring. Cecily is not to be silenced. She deliberately (or is she really so naïve?) misunderstands the comments and links such boredom with agricultural depression.

3 Their actions are amusing because Gwendolen has set herself up to be the fashionable, sophisticated character whilst Cecily is apparently the young country girl, out of touch with London etiquette. Cecily, however, is not to be trampled on and she deliberately acts out the role that Gwendolen has assigned to her. For example, she adds the sugar and gives her visitor an extra large slice of the cake that Gwendolen says is so 'out of fashion'. The visible reactions of each, such as the facial contortions and glares, would be very amusing to the audience.

4 During the dramatic final outbursts Gwendolen stands in a confrontational way. Politeness disappears and the irony of her

deluded self-assessment ('extraordinary sweetness') is a source of humour. Cecily confronts her visitor and is plain in her motives. Gwendolen carries on in her so-called intelligent, but totally mistaken and arrogant assessment of character. She believes she is 'invariably right'. The scene ends on a wonderfully funny, polite note with the careful choice of the verb '*trespassing* on your valuable time' (emphasis added). The audience is fully aware of Cecily's loathing, and her final words that Gwendolen must have other calls to make 'of a similar character' is typical of the nature of this interaction. Cecily does not say openly what she thinks, but the audience is aware of what she implies: that Gwendolen is rude and that she will probably inflict her strong, unwelcome opinions on anyone else that she visits.

5 Wilde uses typical speech features such as politeness strategies ('May I offer you' etc.) and question and answer exchanges, called **adjacency pairs**. For example, Merriman says, 'Shall I lay tea here as usual, Miss?', which is followed by Cecily's response, 'Yes, as usual'. Sentences are elegantly constructed, with no hesitation or reformulation. There is an exaggerated concern for assumed linguistic propriety. This is tidied up dialogue, crafted for effect, and it works very well to convey a humorous but tense comic scene. Food is being used as a **motif**: the tea ceremony symbolises all that is polite, and rather stuffy, in Victorian society. Here are two women apparently conforming to the tedious exchange of polite conversation over tea, but there is subversion and finally the superficial politeness collapses. The whole exchange is vicious.

> ### Key terms
>
> **Adjacency pair:** an utterance by one speaker is followed by a reply from another, making an 'adjacent pair'. The first utterance could be a question or a greeting, and its content points to the kind of reply expected from the second person. So 'What time is it?' might be followed by 'It's 6pm'.
>
> **Motif:** a dominant theme or a recurring symbol.

Comparing the two texts

The 16th century Shakespeare extract differs greatly from the Wilde extract. The mood is sinister and threatening, the action horrific, and of course the language with its framework of blank verse and its lengthier expressive speeches, the 'fearful words', creates the sombre mood. There are some archaisms in the language, but the lexis is relatively simple. Compare this tragic scene with the brittle but humorous interaction between Gwendolen and Cecily. The Wilde play has been called an 'intellectual farce' or a 'comedy of manners' (with echoes of the 18th century plays of Sheridan, such as *The Rivals*). Both extracts are dramatic forms but different genres: comedy and tragedy, but each works effectively on stage to keep an audience interested and keen to know what is going to happen next.

Comparing drama with other genres

Text 21, *Titus Andronicus*, could be compared to:
Text 22 *A Modest Proposal* by Jonathan Swift. A satirical account of how to solve Irish poverty by breeding, eating and selling babies. A prose pamphlet. Black humour, but a serious purpose.
Text 27: 'Workhouse Diets', those kept near starvation level, apocryphal mention of cannibalism. Historical textbook approach reporting the situation.
Text 28: extract from *Oliver Twist*. Food that is not nourishing or sufficient, threats of cannibalism. Prose fiction.
Text 1: 'The Butcher's Shop'. Horrific descriptions, off-putting. Poem genre.

Text 20, *The Importance of Being Earnest*, could be compared to:

Text 3: 'The Sweet Menu'. Etiquette and difficulty of eating alone.

Text 2: 'Eating Out'. Conventions, manners and etiquette of eating out.

Text 13: Restaurant review. Similar tone to Text 20. Blunt criticism of restaurant. Comment on fashions in food.

Text 18: Transcript. A shared meal – very different. Limited conversation, cryptic but with undercurrents.

Text 31: *The Man of Property* by Galsworthy. Account of a meal with much tension, ill-feeling suppressed and politeness forced. Much reliance on dialogue. Similar tone to Text 20.

Comparing Text 22 from *A Modest Proposal* by Jonathan Swift (dramatic prose) with Text 21 *Titus Andronicus*

Before tackling a comparative essay you will need to complete your own analysis of the Swift extract.

Critical response activity

You can find out more about Swift's background and about the contexts of production by completing your own research using the information on page 6 of the Anthology and the following weblink as your starting point: www.victorianweb.org/previctorian/swift/proposal1.html. Then answer the following questions on Text 22: *A Modest Proposal*.

1 Sum up, in note form, the content of each paragraph. This will help you to appreciate how Swift structures his argument.

2 Comment on any aspects of his style which strike you, such as his word choice and grammar (especially syntax).

3 How would you describe the tone of voice that the author takes in this pamphlet?

Practical activity

One of the best ways of becoming familiar with the content and the style of a text is to write a pastiche. (See Chapter 5, page 32 for further details about pastiches.)

Choose an issue that you feel strongly about and offer a solution to the problems caused by the situation. Exaggerate the details, as Swift does, and provide an extreme and ridiculous solution in order to draw attention to the situation. Imitate Swift's sentence structure closely, and follow the order in which he builds a case.

For example, you could take the problems caused by excessive litter and offer a solution, such as making all of the perpetrators eat the litter. You could begin with: 'The number of crisp packets discarded in this country usually amounts to 95 million each day'.

Critical response activity

Preparing for a comparative essay

Compose an outline plan that could be used to answer the following examination-type question:

Food is not always shown to be a source of nourishment and comfort.

Compare two texts from the Anthology that demonstrate this.

In your answer, write about some of the following where appropriate:

- contexts of production and reception
- form and structure
- figurative language
- sound patterning.
- word choice
- grammar
- layout and presentation

(Remember that these prompts are not written in any particular order. You will need to judge their relevance to the text that you are asked to write about as they may *not* all be relevant.)

Commentary

The two texts compared are *A Modest Proposal* and *Titus Andronicus*.
The plan is in note form and shown in a table.

Essay section	A Modest Proposal	Titus Andronicus
Introduction: an overview of each text compared; links made with the food theme.	A satirical pamphlet with grotesque example of babies used as food. Appears serious about cannibalism to solve hunger in Ireland.	The climactic final scenes of the play – contents of the pie revealed. Similarly horrific images, followed by shocking murders.
Form, structure, context (focusing on purpose).	• A prose essay, structured as an argument using spurious but apparently authentic evidence to support cannibalism. • Purpose: to draw attention to problems by using black humour in a supposedly reasonable argument. • 1729: written at a time when Ireland was a colony.	• Play genre dialogue, with a variety of speaking voices. Dominated by lengthy speeches of Titus. Tension carefully built leading to revelations and to murders. • Purpose is to provide a dramatic climax to the play. • First performed about 1590, audience expectations of a revenge tragedy – bloodshed.
Language, including word choice, sound patterning, figurative language, rhetorical devices.	• 18th-century language, so individual words and phrases are often different, e.g. 'Whereof', 'hitherto', 'repine', etc.; expressions such as 'I make no doubt that'. • Use of mathematical and commercial terms to give authenticity – 'computed', 'saleable commodity'. • Use of rhetorical devices: repetition, qualification of speaking voice ('I humbly offer', 'humbly propose'). • Reader infers that often the opposite of what is said is intended (the title is 'modest' but the proposal is extreme).	• Late 16th-century language, so like Swift some words have changed their meaning or fallen out of use, e.g. 'boots', 'forbear', 'strumpet'; expressions like 'draw nigh'. • Different purpose (drama – entertainment) and use of poetic blank verse, so contrasts in word choice and details given; figurative language (Lavinia is compared with goodly summer; classical allusions etc.) More variety in expressions from colloquial ('I would be sure to have all well') to more formal, elaborate phrases ('her spotless chastity' etc.) • Also uses rhetorical devices – tripling: 'enforc'd, stain'd, deflower'd?' • Sound patterning, e.g. onomatopoeia: 'grind'; alliteration: 'Here stands the spring'.
Grammar – especially syntax.	Lengthy, complex sentences with much subordination – main verb often left until later in the sentence. Sounds like a politician's speech. But does use shorter sentences to emphasise a point, such as lines 7–8. Notice word order – adverb precedes verb.	Completely different structure because of different purpose and framework of blank verse. But some sentences are similarly complex (lines 20–29 – Titus talking of Lavinia). Like Swift, there is variety – simple questions such as 'What is your will?'
Tone, mood and overall meaning – with close reference to the food motif.	Biting satire. Tone of voice is mock humble, an apparently serious suggestion about cannibalism. But intention is to shock readers into realising the seriousness of the Irish problems.	• Horrific, bloody scenes. No black humour. Tone of voice of different speakers varies, but mood is tense, with build up to climactic revelations and final murders. • Image of the pie containing heads is memorably grotesque. Food seen as a weapon of revenge – completely distasteful.

Conclusion: Two very different genres with different purposes; one a satire with the aim to draw attention to problems and the other to provide dramatic entertainment. There are some similarities, each aims to shock and each deals with food as a central motif. Swift's image of eating babies is appalling; equally shocking is the thought of two human heads baked in a pie. But the different form and purpose influences language choice and structure. Swift creates a convincing, dramatic speaking voice that describes an extreme solution to a problem and so underlines the seriousness of a situation. Shakespeare provides a dramatic, climax to the play with horrific bloodshed, creating a spectacle for the audience, and some resolution to the issues that have been explored in the drama.

You could now adapt this plan, add your own thoughts and examples and then write the essay in coherent prose, remembering to compare throughout.

Writing a comparative analysis

AQA Examiner's tip

When you are reading textbooks, magazines, newspapers, etc. be alert to the ways in which writers express comparisons. Think about how their sentences are constructed and the ways in which they signal both differences and similarities. Make a note of the sentence structures and vocabulary they use and try to extend your own repertoire so that you can write about comparisons economically and precisely.

Similarities	Differences
similar to	dissimilar to
resembles	is unlike
virtually identical	unlike
is parallel to	diverges from
akin to	differentiated from
correspond to	different from
alike	unalike
compared with	in contrast to
in comparison with	in contradistinction to
likewise	on the other hand
corresponding to	whereas
	however

When you take your Unit 1 examination you will be required to compare texts in both of the compulsory questions on the paper. In Question 1 you will write about two unseen texts and in Question 2 you will choose two of the 33 texts in the Anthology to write about. In the previous chapters of this book you have thought about a wide selection of the texts from the Anthology and considered many of the differences and similarities between them, but in this chapter we are going to explore the idea of comparison further by looking in detail at just one text (Text 12). Text 12 is, in itself, a comparative text. It consists of four reviews of Italian restaurants and so provides much scope for comparing the writers' experiences of the different restaurants. The techniques we shall be exploring in this chapter are applicable to all comparative tasks, including both of the Unit 1 examination tasks. Although we are using a single text as the basis for this chapter, do remember that in the examination you must compare two different texts. You will, however, gain credit for *all* relevant comparative points that you make – including comparisons between texts, and comparisons of different sections within the same text.

■ Text 12: *Olive* magazine article

Text 12 is taken from the BBC food magazine *Olive*, and it consists of the writers' reports on their undercover visits to sample the pizzas at four restaurants. The introductory paragraph of Text 12 sets out the writers' purposes clearly:

> They tried a classic margherita and the most expensive pizza on each menu for fair comparison, and rated the restaurants on atmosphere and service to find out which chain really offers the best value.

The visits to the four restaurants are described in four separate sections, but there is no summary in which the writers make direct comparative comments themselves. Instead, it is left to readers to make their own comparisons on the basis of the writers' comments and their scores out of five for the margherita pizza and for the overall experience.

The language of comparison

Writing a successful comparison requires good planning. You need to know what the focus is for drawing comparisons and pointing out contrasts. You also need to have a repertoire of sentence structures and technical terms that will enable you to write efficiently and clearly about the texts you are comparing. Thinking first about lexis, what are the words and phrases that clearly signal the similarities and differences between two texts that are being compared? The table shows some, but if you use a thesaurus you will find that there are many more.

Some of the words from the table are closely associated with particular grammatical structures, such as:

Whereas Prezzo achieved a total of 10/10, Olive Press was awarded only 2.5.

  (subordinate clause)   (main clause)

Olive Press was awarded only 2.5 **whereas** Prezzo achieved a total of 10/10.

  (main clause)   (subordinate clause)

What is the difference between these two versions that make essentially the same point? The first version places 'whereas' at the beginning of the sentence and this signals that a comparative point is about to be made. The second version does not give the reader a signpost of this sort and the comparative point in the subordinate clause may be seen as less emphatic by the reader. The term **foregrounding** refers to the placing of emphasis on particular words or phrases in a sentence or paragraph. In the first example above, word order is used to foreground the word 'whereas', but there are other foregrounding devices that can be used, such as repetition and various graphological and typographical features (for example use of italics and different font sizes and styles).

Using semicolons

Another useful device for making a comparison or a contrast is to link two similar sentences by using a semicolon. This punctuation mark places the two main clauses in a balanced relationship. Think of a see-saw, with one sentence on the left of the board and another sentence on the right, and the semicolon serving as the fulcrum on which the board is balanced:

| Ask and Piccolino both scored 3/5 for the overall experience; | Olive Press could manage only 2/5. |

▲

Notice the parallel structures on either side of the semicolon. Each clause has as its subject the name of the restaurant, followed by a main verb ('scored' and 'could manage') and a direct object ('3/5' and '2/5'). Notice too that the first clause is more explicit in the choice of main verb and in the use of an adverbial phrase ('for the overall experience') whereas in the second clause it would have been superfluous to repeat this information that also applies to it.

Using semicolons in this way is an effective method of highlighting points of difference, although it is possible to show points of similarity too. Generally, though, it is more economical to highlight similarities by linking the subjects with the conjunction 'and', as in this example:

Both Ask and Prezzo are national chains with more than a hundred branches throughout the country.

Examples of comparative paragraphs

The next examples show some more extended comparative paragraphs based on the material in Text 12. These examples illustrate various comparative techniques, but they are extracts from longer answers. Each paragraph is preceded by a specific question, and in each case you could use the paragraph as a starting point and extend it by adding further points of your own based on a close reading of Text 12.

1 Compare the reviewers' judgements about Olive Press and Prezzo restaurants.

Judged by the quality of their food, the two restaurants were very different. Olive Press achieved a score of 1.5/5 for their pizza margherita whereas Prezzo gained full marks. The mozzarella used in the Olive Press version was described as lacking creaminess and elasticity, and tasting like catering-quality mozzarella rather than the 'good Italian stuff'. By contrast, the Prezzo pizza was 'executed brilliantly' and its mozzarella was the 'best tasting cheese' the reviewer had tasted. Similarly, the pizza bases at Olive Press were 'dry and brittle' at the edges whereas those at Prezzo were 'chewy with a shatteringly crisp perimeter'.

Think about it

A thesaurus is a very useful guide to the synonyms and near-synonyms in English, but it tells you nothing about the level of formality of the words and phrases it lists. You need to take care to consider the appropriateness of words and phrases for the context in which you are writing. For example, which of the following is more appropriate for inclusion in an examination answer?

■ 'Texts A and B are as alike as two peas in a pod'

■ 'Texts A and B exhibit close parallels'.

Key terms

Foregrounding: placing a particular word or phrase within a sentence so as to give it special prominence.

Think about it

The final comment about Olive Press is that the highlight of this Italian restaurant is a bottle of Black Sheep (a beer brewed in North Yorkshire). What does this suggest to you about the reviewer's attitude to the restaurant?

Key terms

Minor sentence: a sentence that contains no main verb, e.g. 'Ready?'; 'So what?'; 'Nonsense!'; 'Two seniors please.' Minor sentences are heavily context dependent, i.e. they are intelligible only in the time and place in which they occur.

2 Compare the reviewers' judgements about quality of service at the restaurants they visited.

The dining experiences were also influenced by the quality of service. At Ask the staff were hard-working and friendly but at Piccolino the reviewer's waiter was described as 'utterly mechanical, even brusque'. Those at Prezzo were 'as charming as the setting' and the waitress was praised as 'refreshingly honest'. The connotations of the words used of Piccolino's standard of service are uncomplimentary: 'mechanical' is bad enough, suggesting as it does a lack of humanity and friendliness, but the adverbial premodifier 'utterly' further emphasises the scale of the problem and presents the restaurant as an unwelcoming and charmless place.

3 Compare the language used in the reviews.

Both the Olive Press and the Piccolino reviews use a similar economical device to signal a question–answer structure. In the case of the Olive Press, a two-word **minor sentence** is used: 'The highlight?' and the answer is immediately given: 'a bottle of Black Sheep ale (£3.95)'. For Piccolino a single word with a question mark is used to focus on the less successful aspects of the restaurant: 'Niggles?' and the rest of the paragraph specifies what they were. In a review of this sort where space is limited the writer is able to make his points succinctly. 'The Highlight?' and 'Niggles?' (both with question marks) serve almost as subheadings and allow the discourse to move forward in a direct and clear way.

Commentary

1 Notice in the first example how the opening sentence sets out the broad basis for the comparison (quality of food), whereas the following sentences refer to specific aspects that explain the differences in quality, with textual evidence to support the comparisons. The paragraph makes comparative evaluative comments about the pizzas and provides the necessary textual evidence in support of these comments.

2 Notice how the opening sentence focuses on quality of service but the word 'also' acts as a link between this and what has come before. Notice too how textual evidence in the form of direct quotations from Text 12 are embedded within the comments. The final sentence focuses on how the writer uses language to convey his evaluations of service at Piccolino.

3 Notice how the opening sentence points to a similarity between two reviews in terms of the way in which information is structured. The next two sentences give specific explanations and illustrations to support the general point made in the first sentence, and the final sentence comments on the effectiveness of the discourse structure of the text.

Linking evaluative comments and textual evidence

In the second example above, the connotation of the word 'mechanical' carries a strong evaluative message for the reader. Unless we have good reason to doubt the good faith of the writer we are probably inclined to accept his or her judgement, especially if the basis for the opinion is also presented to us. If the criteria for evaluations are set out clearly we can judge whether the writer's comments are fair or unfair. Sometimes, however, writers and speakers use evaluative language without letting us know on what basis they have arrived at their judgements. Opinions of this sort should arouse the suspicion of the reader or listener and you should avoid making unsupported assertions in your examination answers.

It is vital that your comments about the texts in the Anthology are linked with clear information about the criteria you apply and the evidence you can offer to support your analysis. Look again at the sample paragraphs 1–3 to see how the relationship between basis/evaluation/evidence is organised.

Another possible way of organising your material is to move from specific textual details to a general conclusion, for example:

> 'The writer uses a sequence of adverbs and adjectives (laughably small, vaguely fishy, lacklustre, dry and brittle), which have a strongly negative cumulative effect, suggesting that this is not the place to go for good Italian food.'

A photograph accompanies the review of each of the restaurants. Because these images have an important role helping to convey an impression of the character of each restaurant, a successful analysis also needs to assess their impact on readers of the text. For example:

> 'The Ask photograph shows a customer and a waitress smiling at each other, yet the Olive Press photograph shows only a building. This contrast helps to create very different impressions of each restaurant, the first focusing on staff and customers interacting happily in the restaurant whereas the Olive Press image is impersonal, showing the façade of a large building with closed doors and not a person in sight.'

Or (and this example is just for fun!):

> 'Prezzo uses impossibly high bar stools, whereas Piccolino seems to attract shrubs in large pots rather than paying customers.'

Critical response activity

Practise writing comparative sentences by following these suggestions:

1. Select two of the photographs in Text 12 and write a comparative sentence about the visual messages they convey.

2. Write a few comparative sentences that highlight contrasts between any two of the four restaurants, drawing your evidence from the reviews. Try to use different words and sentence structures to present the contrast in each of your examples.

Critical response activity

The two writers of Text 12 use some entertaining and amusing phrases, such as the wordplay in 'Pizzas … lack pizazz' (Olive Press). From the review of each restaurant select two examples of phrases that you think are particularly effective and explain what you think makes each example effective.

AQA Examiner's tip

Train yourself to look for significant detail in texts – details of language, details of content, details of design, details of structure – but always relate them to the way the text as a whole conveys its overall message to its audience. Always focus your answer according to the precise requirements of the question.

AQA Examiner's tip

The examination questions ask you to compare texts, but there are often valuable comparative points to be made about the language used within different sections of the same text. Remember the Jonathan Crisp and Salty Dog texts (Texts 23 and 24) for example, and look at the advertisement for Grape Nuts (Text 25) for a contrast between the opening and the closing paragraphs.

In the examination you will have to write about two different texts, but you will gain credit for making effective comparative points both *within* and *between* texts.

▇ Answering the examination questions

Chapters 9 and 10 provide examples of the sorts of questions you are likely to face in the examination. Chapter 9 deals with Question 1, in which you are presented with two unseen texts on the theme of food. Chapter 10 deals with Question 2, in which you have to choose two of the 33 texts in the Anthology that are suitable for answering the question you are faced with. It is, of course, impossible to predict which texts you will be able to use for your Question 2 answer. Depending on the exact nature of the question, some texts will be more suitable than others and some texts may be completely inappropriate. The best general advice is to examine Question 2 carefully and then draw up a shortlist of texts that you think would be relevant. From that list you then need to select the two texts that you think will enable you to produce your best possible answer. You need to manage your time carefully, given that you have to prepare and write two essays in 1 hour 45 minutes.

Critical response activity

The following questions are examples of what you might expect to be set on the Anthology texts in the Unit 1 examination:

*Question 2, Example **A***:

> Compare two texts from the Anthology which deal with the experience of eating out in a restaurant.

*Question 2, Example **B***:

> Compare two texts from the Anthology in which the spoken voice features prominently.

In the examination, Question 2 is followed by seven bullet points outlining aspects that you are expected to consider as part of your answer. See Chapter 10 for more examples of questions in their full form.

For each of the Question 2 examples above decide:

1   What are key words, so that your decisions are focused precisely on what the question asks you to do.

2   Which of the 33 texts in the Anthology could be included on a shortlist as relevant to an examination answer.

3   Which two of the texts on your shortlist would provide you with the best opportunity to make a range of points about their similarities and differences.

When you have done this, compare your decisions about the shortlists with those suggested below. Try to resist the temptation to read the comments below until you have made your own decisions about which texts to select for Examples A and B.

Commentary

Question 2, Example A

Relevant texts include:

Text 2 'Eating Out'	Text 3 'The Sweet Menu'
Text 12 'How We Did It' (restaurant reviews)	Text 13 'Restaurants'
Text 19 Transcript	

Other texts that deal with eating a meal would not be relevant because their settings are not restaurants. For example, Text 33 describes a feast served to academics in a university dining hall; Text 31 describes a private dinner served in a country house; Text 29 describes the breakfast served at a rectory; Text 27 describes the food served to inmates of workhouses; and Text 26 describes the food served in working-class homes in the 1920s and 1930s.

One other text in the Anthology (Text 14) is partially relevant but it would be a risky choice for this question because it would force a student who chose it to write almost exclusively about the menu itself and the language used to describe the dishes, which is only a limited part of 'the experience of eating out'. It would be difficult to keep the answer relevant to the question.

Question 2, Example B

Relevant texts include:

All of the poetry texts (especially 1–4 and 6)	Text 9 'Why we all need to eat red meat'
Text 17 Transcript of Nigella Lawson	Text 18 Transcript
Text 19 Transcript	The drama texts (20–21)
Text 22 from *A Modest Proposal*	Text 28 from *Oliver Twist*
Text 30 from *Little Grey Rabbit*	Text 31 from *The Man of Property*

The poetry texts all have some characteristics of the speaking voice of the poet, although this is probably least evident in Texts 5 and 7. Text 9 is a newspaper article placed on a website, but the writer's style is direct and includes informal expressions ('Well, calm down, everyone!'). The transcripts are records of actual speech and the drama extracts are scripted representations of speech, and the last three texts include dialogue within the prose narrative. The most surprising text to include in this list is perhaps the extract from *A Modest Proposal*; however, at times it has a strong sense of being a prepared speech ('I shall now therefore humbly propose my own thoughts'). The contrast between the reasonable voice and the shocking proposals is an important aspect of Swift's rhetorical method.

9 The unseen texts question (Question 1)

This chapter covers:

- how to approach unseen texts on the theme of 'food glorious food'

- practice questions in the style that you can expect in the examination

- how to ensure that your answers target Assessment Objectives 1, 2 and 3 successfully.

Practical activity

The four Assessment Objectives bullet points on this page are expressed in language that is not taken directly from the AOs in the published specification. Your task is to say which of the AOs below relates most closely to each of the bullet points. Remember: there are only three AOs but there are four bullet points, which means that two bullets will apply to one AO.

AO1 tests your ability to select and apply relevant concepts and approaches from integrated linguistic and literary study.

AO2 tests your ability to demonstrate detailed critical understanding in analysing the ways in which structure, form and language shape meanings in a range of spoken and written texts.

AO3 tests your ability to use integrated approaches to explore relationships between texts, analysing and evaluating the significance of contextual factors in their production and reception.

In the examination – Question 1

The unseen texts on 'food glorious food'

The first of the two compulsory questions in Unit 1 relates to two unseen texts that are printed in the examination paper. Because the topic of food is so broad, you must be ready to think carefully about how to adapt your knowledge of the particular meanings, forms and features to previously unseen texts. Do not be intimidated by this. The format of the questions will be familiar and the texts will have been carefully selected as having some good opportunities for you to find points of similarity and points of difference. If you read the two texts carefully and remember to apply the analytical techniques that you have developed during the course, you will be able to write a comprehensive and successful comparative answer.

Timings

You will have 1 hour and 45 minutes to complete both questions in the Unit 1 examination. This should allow you plenty of time to read the unseen texts closely and thoughtfully. You should devote about 40 minutes to preparing and writing your answer to Question 1.

The Assessment Objectives

You will be marked according to the following criteria:

- whether you can write relevantly in response to the question

- whether you can comment accurately and insightfully about the ways in which meanings are created and conveyed in the two texts

- whether you can demonstrate both linguistic and literary understanding of the texts

- whether you can maintain a comparative approach in your writing about the two texts.

Commentary

The first bullet point links to AO1, which refers to the need to select and apply relevant concepts and approaches. The second bullet point focuses on meaning, as does AO2. The third bullet point refers to literary and linguistic understanding, which is similar to the final words of AO1 – 'integrated linguistic and literary study'. Finally, the fourth bullet point refers to the importance of maintaining a comparative approach, and this is echoed in AO3, where it uses the words 'explore relationships between texts'.

How to approach Question 1

The following steps will help you to successfully respond to the question:

1 **Understand the question**. The vital first step is to make certain that you understand what the question is asking you to do. If you rush into writing your answer with only a vague sense of what you need to do, your answer is likely to be seriously flawed.

Focusing carefully on the wording of the question will enable you to understand exactly what you need to concentrate on in your reading and analysis of the two unseen texts. You have limited time in which to prepare and write your answer so it is essential to concentrate on what is most relevant to the question.

2 **Understand the context**. Before you begin the detailed reading of the two texts, think about the contextual information that is given about each passage. For example, you might be told that one extract is from a novel and the other is from a newspaper article. Cont... information of this sort should guide your analysis and your re... as a reader.

3 **Read both texts carefully**. Make sure you consider the intend... audiences for the two passages, the writer's apparent purpose... ways in which the texts are presented and structured, and the... in which particular features of language are used. Make notes... the points that you find. You are, of course, allowed to annot... the unseen texts printed on the examination paper and you s... certainly do so.

4 **Choosing what to compare**. As you read the two texts you ... probably realise that there are key points of similarity and k... of difference. You need to select a manageable number of m... and write about them in some detail rather than produce a ... superficial answer that tries to cover more ground than is s... the time available.

Although there is no way of predicting which unseen texts yo... encounter in the examination, there are some important points that are predictable:

■ the topic area for your Unit 1 examination is food
■ the wording of the question does not change from one examination series to the next
■ there will be two unseen texts to analyse and write about
■ you will be assessed according to AOs 1, 2 and 3.

The wording of Question 1

The wording of Question 1 will follow this pattern:

Text A is [explanation of source/context].

Text B is [explanation of source/context].

Compare the ways in which the texts achieve their purposes.

You should compare:

■ *how the texts are structured and how they present their material*
■ *how the purposes and contexts of the texts influence language choices.*

The wording of the task does not change from year to year, but the unseen texts do, and this question is designed specifically to test your ability to analyse unseen texts. The standard wording ensures that all students are tested in exactly the same way, so when you enter the examination room you should be completely familiar with the wording of Question 1. This should enable you to focus initially on the contextual information given about the unseen texts and then to use that information in an active, thoughtful way as you read the texts themselves.

■ Some practice questions

The following questions and text pairings are in the style of those you will face in Question 1 in the examination.

1 Fish and chips

Text A is taken from the website of Simpsons Fish and Chips, a small family-owned business with shops in Cheltenham, Bristol and Chepstow.

Text B is an extract from *Cod: A Biography of the Fish that Changed the World* by Mark Kurlansky.

Compare the ways in which the texts achieve their purposes.

You should compare:

■ how the texts are structured and how they present their material

■ how the purposes and contexts of the texts influence language choices.

Text A

Simpsons
fish & chips

Cheltenham 01242 521 964
Chepstow   01291 620 294
Bristol   01454 201 110

▼ home

▼ about us

▼ cheltenham

▼ chepstow

▼ bristol

▼ our fish & chips

▼ competitions

▼ latest news

▼ useful links

▼ contact us

Our Batter

Our batter is all natural and contains no MSG, no salt, no bulking agents and no artificial flavouring or colours.

Our Fish & Chips

Our uniqueness is our quality.

We are a traditional fish and chip shop with traditional food but at a very high standard. Everyday we are told by customers "*this the best fish and chips I've ever had*", one even added "*and I'm 83!*"

▼ All our cod and haddock is skinless and boneless.
▼ We also fry in pure groundnut oil which makes everything lighter and crispier.

Our policies for food

We have many policies, the main one being that we generally cook fish to order, unless it's very busy, to guarantee freshness. Our batter has to be thin and crispy. All food is probed to make sure it's to the correct temperature before it's ready to serve. Our chips are cooked fresh often as we keep it as tight as possible, if we think they are past their best they get thrown away.

Our fish

Our main fish is the best quality frozen at sea cod, they come in huge fillets and we thaw them to cut them into portions every morning.

Frozen at sea cod is much fresher than 'wet fish' which is fish that isn't frozen, most people don't call this 'fresh fish' anymore as it is impossible to keep this fish fresh when it has to travel from the sustainable stocks which is very important to us. Our supplier, T Quality, demands that from 'Sea to Tea', fish should be traceable back to the catchments area, vessel and operator. So each box of fish we buy clearly shows the area that particular catch was from and the boat name, it even has a packer number inside so we can trace the person who packed it up for us!

Our cod and haddock is mainly from around Iceland and the Barent sea. We are told the fish is frozen within 4 hours of being caught, so when we get it, it hasn't dried up and is still wonderfully flaky.

Our chips

Our potatoes are bought from local British farmers, each shop has a different supplier so there are less food miles.

We test all the types of potato the supplier has throughout the year and choose the one we think is best at the time. So it could be the faithful maris piper, but if we think the sugar content is too high we will transfer to markies and so on.

Text B

38 § A Fish Tale

But to the commercial fisherman, there have always been five kinds of gadiform: the Atlantic cod, the haddock, the pollock, the whiting, and the hake. Increasingly, a sixth gadiform must be added to the list, the Pacific cod, *Gadus macrocephalus*, a smaller version of the Atlantic cod whose flesh is judged of only slightly lesser quality.

The Atlantic cod, however, is the largest, with the whitest meat. In the water, its five fins unfurl, giving an elegant form that is streamlined by a curving white stripe up the sides. It is also recognizable by a square rather than forked tail and a curious little appendage on the chin, which biologists think is used for feeling the ocean floor.

The smaller haddock has a similar form but is charcoal-colored on the back where the cod is spotted browns and ambers; it also has a black spot on both sides above the pectoral fin. The stripe on a haddock is black instead of white. In New England, there is a traditional explanation for this difference. There, cod is sometimes referred to as "the sacred cod". In truth, this is because it has earned New Englanders so many sacred dollars. But according to New England folklore, it was the fish that Christ multiplied to feed the masses. In the legend, Satan tried to do the same thing, but since his hands were burning

39 § *With Mouth Open Wide*

hot, the fish wriggled away. The burn mark of Satan's thumb and forefinger left black stripes; hence the haddock.

This story illustrates the difference, not only in stripes but in status, between cod and haddock. British and Icelandic fishermen only reluctantly catch haddock after their cod quotas are filled, because cod always brings a better price. Yet Icelanders prefer eating haddock and rarely eat cod except dried. Asked why this is so, Reykjavik chef Úlfar Eysteinsson said, "We don't eat money".

The stars are *tout morue*, and cod is money; haddock is simply food. The Nova Scotians, true to their name-sakes, prefer haddock, even for fish-and-chips, which would be considered a travesty in Newfoundland and virtually a fraud in the south of England. In the north of England, as in Scotland, haddock is preferred.

*Tout morue is the French name for codfish.

2 Indian spices

Text A on the following page is taken from *Ghost Train to the Eastern Star*, a travel book by Paul Theroux. In this extract Theroux and Kapoorchand (whose first language is not English) meet while on an overnight train journey in India.

Text B is an extract from *Orchards in the Oasis: Recipes, Travels and Memories* by Josceline Dimbleby.

Compare the ways in which the texts achieve their purposes.

You should compare:

▓ how the texts are structured and how they present their material

▓ how the purposes and contexts of the texts influence language choices.

Text A

Kapoorchand seemed eager to discuss the life of the soul. Perhaps because he had just finished eating, he talked about the spiritual aspects of food.

'Onions and garlic are worst,' he said. 'They make a desire for sex. And they cause angerness.'

'I did not know that.'

'My friend when he travels without wife never eats onions.' He was enumerating vegetables on his fingers. 'Carrots. Root vegetables. I don't eat because it is killing the living plant. I eat tops only.'

'Potatoes?'

'Some people eat. But for me – no. So many live things can be found on a potato.'

'Live things, such as …?'

'Bacteria and moulds. Why should they be killed because of me?'

For this reason, Jains habitually wore masks, so as not to inhale any gnats that might be hovering near their open mouths, and they swept at the

surface of water to disperse – what? Water bugs? Mosquito larvae? – before they drank. It was a strict interpretation of the Do Not Kill stricture: nothing must be killed, and that included flies and mould.

'Fruit is good, but … bananas can be tricky. It depends on time of day.' Up went his admonitory finger. 'Banana is gold in morning. Silver in afternoon. Iron in evening. One should not eat bananas in evening. Also, no yoghurt in evening, but yoghurt in morning is beneficial.

'Indian food is spicy, though,' I said.

'Not beneficial. Chillies and pickle make angerness. They increase cruel nature.'

I could see that he enjoyed putting me in the know, because there is a freight of detail in Indian life – an ever-present cargo of dogma, of strictures, of lessons, of distinctions – that turns Indians into monologuers.

*Jain: Mr Kapoorchand follows the Jain faith.

Text B

One morning, later in our journey, we saw a large elephant and several groups walking along the road ahead of us before turning off towards an extensive area of multi-coloured tents. Our driver Kuman told us that these people were on a pilgrimage to Palitana, organised and paid for by rich Jains. There were eight hundred pilgrims of all ages. They walked barefoot for eighteen kilometres a day starting at 5am, though the tents, bedding, luggage, food and cooks went ahead of them in trucks to the next overnight stop. And they had the occasional day of rest, such as the one we had stumbled on. We were received enthusiastically by a group of Jain priests, female as well as male, who invited us to lunch. In one enormous tent we found a scene of extreme jollity and loud laughter; hundreds of people squatted in long rows at low tables eating Gujarati thalis with gusto. Like many westerners I find it hard to squat comfortably on the ground and I moved about awkwardly, next to a large lady, who was totally at ease. But the thali was well worth the discomfort.

On large leaves, sewn together with grass, were fine slices of sweet purple onions, scarlet tomatoes, slices of red carrot, raw beetroot, cucumbers and sprouting mug dal. And tiny dishes were continually refilled with mung dal curry; charged aubergines and sweet tomatoes; a red chilli and garlic chutney; a mildly spiced puree of green vegetables; rice, lentils and peas with a burnt, crispy top; and chickpeas fried with salt, peanut flour and chilli.

Most savoury dishes in Gujarat are slightly sweetened, but there is a great variety of sweet dishes too, eaten at the same time as the savoury ones, not afterwards. That day we had *sukri*, made from wheat, palm sugar and ghee, and syrupy golden *jelebis*. White buffalo butter was served in clay pots, and we drank buffalo buttermilk sprinkled with salt and cumin.

As we left, feeling as large as these hefty pilgrims, Kuman told us that he often drove Jains and that they were always very cheerful.

3 Food as fuel

Text A is taken from a non-fiction book, *Science*, by Charles Taylor and Stephen Pople.

Text B is an extract from *The Year 1000*, subtitled *What Life was Like at the Turn of the First Millennium*.

Compare the ways in which the texts achieve their purposes.

You should compare:

■ how the texts are structured and how they present their material

■ how the purposes and contexts of the texts influence language choices.

Text A

THE FUEL FACTORY

Most engines run on only one type of fuel. It is usually petrol or diesel oil. The human engine can run on a wide variety of fuels – bread, potatoes, pizzas, spaghetti, eggs, rice, chocolate biscuits – whatever food you happen to fancy.

Most of the foods you eat cannot be directly used by the body as fuel. First, they must be processed by the body's 'fuel factory'. They must be changed into substances like glucose which will dissolve and can be carried by the blood. Changing food into a dissolved form is called digestion.

Digestion starts in your mouth when food is chewed and mixed with saliva. But it mainly takes place in the stomach and small intestine. These are part of the alimentary canal, or gut – a long tube which runs right through your body from mouth to anus. Parts of the gut are coiled up, but if it were stretched out it would be over 7 metres long.

As food passes along the gut, chemicals called enzymes get to work on it and change it into a dissolved form. Liquid substances, like glucose, then pass through the wall of the gut and into the bloodstream. This process is called absorption. It mainly takes place in the small intestine.

Some of the materials in food are not digested: the fibre in vegetables and fruits, for example. These, mixed with some unwanted water, pass out of the anus when you use the toilet. Fibre may be wasted by the body, but it is still an important part of a healthy diet. It provides bulk which helps to keep food moving along the gut and prevents constipation.

CHEWING CHANGES

Bread contains starch, which does not dissolve in water. When you chew a piece of bread, it is mixed with saliva. This contains an enzyme that changes starch into glucose sugar – which does dissolve in water. Changing starch into glucose in your mouth is the first stage of digestion.

Try chewing a piece of bread very slowly for about five minutes. The taste should get sweeter as more and more starch is changed into glucose.

FUEL IN STORE

When you eat a meal, your digestive system gets to work on the food and produces plenty of glucose – the body's main fuel. This fuel ends up in the blood, but you cannot normally use all of it straight away. Much of it must be put into storage.

Storing fuel is one of the jobs done by the liver. It takes unwanted glucose from the blood and changes it into a substance called glycogen, which it can store. Later, if you need extra fuel, the liver changes glycogen back into glucose. Muscles also store glycogen, which can readily be changed into glucose as and when required.

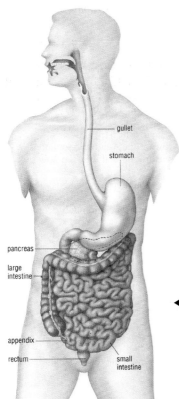

◀◀ The alimentary canal, or gut, runs from the mouth to the anus. In the stomach and small intestine, food is digested – it is broken down into a form which will dissolve. In the small intestine, dissolved food is absorbed by the blood. In the large intestine, much of the remaining water is absorbed. This leaves a semi-solid waste containing undigested food.

Diagram labels: gullet, stomach, pancreas, large intestine, appendix, rectum, small intestine

Text B

Meat was the principal ingredient of an Anglo-Saxon feast – large spit-roast joints of beef being considered the best treat. Mutton was not a particular delicacy. Wulfstan's memorandum of estate management described mutton as a food for slaves, and pork seems also to have been considered routine.

The relatively small amounts of fat on all these meats would be viewed by modern nutritionists with quite a kindly eye. Saturated fat, the source of cholesterol with its related contemporary heath problems, is a problem of the intensively reared factory-farmed animals of recent years, with their overabundant "scientific" diets and their lack of exercise. All Anglo-Saxon animals were free range, and the Anglo-Saxons would have been shocked at the idea of ploughing land to produce animal feed. Ploughland was for feeding humans. So farm animals were lean and rangey, their

meat containing three times as much protein as fat. With modern, intensively reared animals that ratio is often reversed.

Poultry was considered a luxury food, and it was also recognised as a therapeutic diet for invalids, particularly in broth form. Old English recipe and remedy books show that in the year 1000 chicken soup was already renowned for its soothing and restorative powers. As well as chickens, an Anglo-Saxon feast might feature ducks, geese, pigeons, and various forms of game birds – with venison the most highly prized game of all.

Aelfric's schoolroom colloquy is eloquent on the subject of fish, which his "Fisherman" describes himself catching by net, bait, hook, and basket.

*Colloquy means a discussion

4 Market scenes

Text A is taken from Robert Genn's website for artists.

Text B is an extract from 'Goblin Market', a poem by Christina Rossetti.

Compare the ways in which the texts achieve their purposes.

You should compare:

- how the texts are structured and how they present their material
- how the purposes and contexts of the texts influence language choices.

Text A

http://clicks.robertgenn.com/turkish-market.php   Google

Dear Artist,
In Istanbul the great marketplace is jammed. Arm in arm the shoppers come, jostled, impeded and pressed forward by the throng. Noisy and competitive, it's a fluid masterpiece of diversity and the side-by-side offering of similar products and services. An observer might notice a few things:

Beans and lentils piled to dangerous heights get more attention than beans and lentils in half-empty bins.

Precious items like saffron and caviar become more precious when put into fine and delicate packaging.

Kebabs, chestnuts and olives get more attention when they are actively moved around.

Turkish delights get more interest in shops where there is a greater variety to choose from.

Moving a big bag of Turkish coffee to the front of a shop shows something about the shopkeeper's attitude.

Passersby learn to respect the restoration of shoes when they watch cobblers at work.

The distinctive and pleasantly memorable odour of bread is advertising enough for this product.

Shopkeepers who appear to be friendly and seem to have a lot of friends appear to be more prosperous.

The lamb catches attention by being actively and enthusiastically sliced. People become hungry when they see

the lamb being energetically sliced on the spit.

Melons, pomegranates, cabbages and all manner of eggs are snapped up because they are fresh.

There is a movement toward the Anatolian tomatoes because the word has gone around that they are now in season.

Workers and shopkeepers who appear to be busy tend to be truly busier than those who are relaxed at their work.

People flock to certain produce because other people are flocking to it.

Some customers show off to their friends by buying extreme numbers of peppers and pimentos.

Some customers try to show good will and personal well being by paying the highest of asking prices.

Ottoman carpets are at their most appealing when you get your hands and feet on them.

Bonitos and mullets are most acceptable when they are still actively flopping.

Both the fishermen and the fish mongers are persistent and put in long hours.

The most desirable stuff is often tucked away at the back of the shop.

Best regards,
Robert

Text B

Morning and evening	Morns that pass by,
Maids heard the goblins cry:	Fair eves that fly;
'Come buy our orchard fruits,	Come buy, come buy;
Come buy, come buy:	Our grapes fresh from the vine,
Apples and quinces,	Pomegranates full and fine,
Lemons and oranges,	Dates and sharp bullaces,
Plump unpecked cherries,	Rare pears and greengages,
Melons and raspberries,	Damsons and bilberries,
Bloom-down-cheeked peaches,	Taste them and try:
Swart-headed mulberries,	Currants and gooseberries,
Wild free-born cranberries,	Bright-fire-like barberries,
Crab-apples, dewberries,	Figs to fill your mouth,
Pine-apples, blackberries,	Citrons from the South,
Apricots, strawberries –	Sweet to tongue and sound to eye,
All ripe together	Come buy, come buy.'
In summer weather –	

Extract from 'Goblin Market', by Christina Rossetti

An approach to Question 1: Fish and chips

Remember that it is not enough simply to mention relevant points. Making a large number of points does not guarantee high marks if those points are not explained and illustrated effectively. It is well worth taking time to study past question papers and the mark scheme on the AQA website. The following link www.aqa.org.uk/qualifications/a-level/english-and-media/english-language-and-literature-b.php will take you to the part of the website where you can select 'Key materials' and look at past papers and mark schemes for all of the available examination series.

Understanding the question

Text A is taken from the website of Simpsons Fish and Chips, a small family-owned business with shops in Cheltenham, Bristol and Chepstow.

Text B is an extract from *Cod: A Biography of the Fish that Changed the World* by Mark Kurlansky.

Compare the ways in which the texts achieve their purposes.

You should compare:

- how the texts are structured and how they present their material
- how the purposes and contexts of the texts influence language choices.

The points made in the table overleaf illustrate in some detail the sorts of comment that might be made about the texts. These points are known as 'indicative content' – that is, an indication for examiners of the sorts of points that candidates are likely to make in their answers. The indicative content sections of mark schemes do not list every possible point that might be made, and examiners are required to be receptive to all points made by candidates, and to judge those points 'on their merits'. In other words, examiners do not approach your work with a predetermined picture of the perfect answer and mark you down according to how far you fall short of that answer. Instead, they evaluate your answer according to the criteria in the mark scheme; they mark positively, rewarding appropriately the relevant points you make and the ways in which you use evidence to support your points.

	Text A Simpsons fish and chips	Text B *Cod: A Biography …*
Audience	Readers who search online for information about fish and chip shops in the Cheltenham/Bristol/Chepstow area; existing customers who want to find out more about the company and its policies.	Readers interested in finding out about the cod species and its ecology, as well as its commercial and gastronomic aspects.
Purpose	To *inform* readers about the company's approach to: • sourcing its fish and potatoes • ensuring that it supplies only freshly cooked food. By implication, to *persuade* readers of the superior quality of the fish and chips sold by Simpsons shops. This is achieved by *explaining* why its policies result in fresher flavour and texture.	To *inform* readers about cod, as well as other gadiform species, including their distinctive appearance, their commercial value and consumers' regional preferences.
Structure and presentation	Within a narrow black border, there are distinct sections: • the company name is prominently shown top right, and a photograph of a shop counter is shown top left • a navigation menu for access to other pages appears on the left, as well as information about the batter used and a distinctive logo • under the main heading 'Our Fish & Chips', there are four sections, each with its own subheading, giving information about these aspects of the company's business.	The text is not distinctive in terms of design and graphology. It consists of five paragraphs, dealing with: • identification of five kinds of gadiform • characteristics of Atlantic cod • characteristics of haddock, and the folklore account of the haddock's markings • explanation of greater commercial value of cod • regional and national basis of cod/haddock preferences. Cohesive devices create a strong sense of development as different aspects are explained.
Language	• Use of repeated first person personal and possessive pronouns (we, our) in headings, subheadings and main body of text. • Frequent use of positive evaluative language (very high standard, guarantee freshness, correct temperature, best quality, wonderfully flaky, best at the time, faithful maris piper (sic), all natural). • Indicative mood is used throughout, which reflects the main purpose of informing readers about the company's policies and approaches. • Style is generally at the mid-point of the formality/informality continuum, with 'it's' and 'don't' used occasionally; the use of customer endorsements in the opening paragraph personalises the address to readers. • The punctuation of sentence boundaries is sometimes inaccurate, with commas used instead of full stops, and the proper names Maris Piper and Markies are not capitalised. • Some complex sentences with mainly adverbial clauses. • Some extended adjectival premodification (the best quality frozen at sea).	• Informative, factual explanatory language predominates. • Some scientific lexis is used (gadiform, *Gadus macrocephalus*, appendage, pectoral), but non-specialist terms also occur (curious little), and reference is also made to folklore/bible story and a French word for codfish is given, possibly to remind readers of the French cultural links between France and Canada. • Precise descriptions of the features distinguishing cod from haddock are given. • An Icelandic chef is quoted to explain the difference between haddock (as food) and cod (as money). • Frequent use of complex sentence structures, but simple and compound structures also used.

When you write your answer on these or other text pairings your comments on audience and purpose do not need to be extensive. Normally they can be made quite concisely so that you can move on to the more detailed analysis of structure and presentation and language. These are the two areas that provide you with the most scope to demonstrate your ability to engage in purposeful analysis and comparison.

For the other Question 1 specimens included in this chapter, an indicative content section of the mark scheme is not provided, but the practical activity invites you to take on the role of a senior examiner who sets the questions and writes the mark schemes.

Practical activity

Your task is to put yourself in the position of the senior examiners who choose text pairings for this examination and then produce indicative content for the mark schemes. The Fish and chips mark scheme provides the model that you should follow for creating the indicative content section for one of the other specimen questions, 2 to 5.

You can do this task individually or as part of a small group. Follow this sequence:

1. Choose one of the other text pairings that you would like to work on.

2. Read the texts carefully to gain an overview of each one and of the main similarities and differences between them.

3. Draw up a grid like the one shown above for the Fish and chips text. Dealing with each text in turn, fill in the grid to include points about:

    a   audience

    b   purpose

    c   structure and presentation

    d   language.

When you have had plenty of practice in thinking about approaching texts in this way, you will be well prepared to think about your examination texts in the same way so that you can prepare your answer in a focused and efficient way.

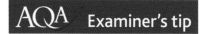

Examiner's tip

Here is some useful advice based on recent examiner feedback on Question 1.

1   Be aware that the unseen texts can be of any genre, spoken or written, as long as they reflect the theme of the current Anthology.

2   You must compare the texts; if you do not you will not be able to gain the marks available for comparison.

3   Your comparison needs to:

    a   be planned, structured and backed up by evidence

    b   compare significant features of a text rather than trivial ones (e.g. commenting on the nature of textual cohesion in the texts is much more relevant than stating that one text has six paragraphs but the other has seven).

4   Avoid writing general introductions and conclusions. Move directly into specific analysis of the two texts and specific evaluative and explanatory comments.

Now read the following answer to Question 1 based on Fish and chips. There are comments beside the answer that will help you to identify its strengths and weaknesses. (You might prefer to read the commentary answer straight through first, and then re-read it looking at the examiner's comments as well.)

Sample response

Text A and Text B are both about fish but in appearance, content and language the two texts are very different because of their contrasting contexts and purposes. Text A is taken from the website of a family-owned fish and chip shop but Text B is from a non-fiction book. The main title in Text B is 'Cod' but there is a subtitle 'the Fish that Changed the World', which is intriguing. The fish and chip shop website has a fairly simple purpose, which is to advertise their food, and this is done mainly by stressing the high quality of their fish, batter and potatoes, as well as their cooking processes.

Starts with comparative comment, pointing out similarities but focusing more on differences of genre, purpose and audience.

Accurately contrasts the contexts and purposes of each text, giving an initial overview as a basis for more detailed comparative analysis.

<table>
<tr><td>

Relates the presentation of the material in each text to its specific purpose and audience. Refers to distinctive design features and content of both texts, and refers to some aspects of language use.

</td><td>

The two texts are different visually, with Text A using a range of different design features and Text B presented in five ordinary paragraphs of text. This difference relates to the different purposes and audiences for each text. The book extract is aimed at serious audiences that want to find out about many aspects of the cod. The extract mentions commercial fishing and uses the scientific-sounding word 'gadiform', as well as describing other members of the cod family, and it mentions New England folklore about the cod, with a religious reference and also its commercial value.

</td></tr>
<tr><td>

Interprets range of purposes relevant to each text on the basis of contextual and content features. Uses precise description of Text A features and summarises main content elements of Text B to draw sound inferences about purposes.

</td><td>

The Simpsons website is probably for people who do an internet search for fish and chip shops in their local area, as well as regular customers who might be attracted to the website because of the competitions mentioned in the navigation bar.

The Text B writer's purpose is to inform his readers. He covers a wide range of aspects, and the words from the title 'the Fish that Changed the World' make a big claim that the extract does not really explain. The Simpsons website also gives us information (in four main sections with red subheadings) about its policies, its fish and its chips, but it goes further to try to persuade readers that they put quality first, so the website tries to persuade and inform at the same time.

</td></tr>
<tr><td>

Focuses on aspects of structure and organisation, with some discussion of specific language points in each text.

</td><td>

Both texts are clearly structured. Text B tells us about members of the gadiform family (but not what 'gadiform' means) and the differences between cod and haddock, including a folklore account of their different markings. The last two paragraphs go on to explain the different commercial value of cod and haddock, and consumers' preferences. Simpsons have used a web designer and the result is professional-looking with a photograph of their fish and chips. The red subheadings all begin with the personal pronoun 'Our' (uniqueness is our quality/ policies for food/fish/chips) and the text then explains what is good about Simpsons under each heading.

</td></tr>
<tr><td>

Comments on the semantic impact of some key words in Text A; identifies some errors in language use but avoids exaggerating their significance within the website context.

</td><td>

The language of the Simpsons text focuses on explaining what is good about their business – with words like 'high standard', 'freshness', 'wonderfully flaky', 'best'. Occasionally it seems to have some errors (some missing capitals and full stops). The language is accessible to a general audience, and it succeeds in communicating Simpsons' messages very effectively. Text B, however, uses more unfamiliar language at times, including the Latin name for the Pacific cod and 'tout morue', the French name for cod. The sentence structures of Text B are not particularly complicated but the subject matter is more demanding than that of Text A. In their different ways both texts succeed in informing readers and making the content interesting.

</td></tr>
<tr><td>

Concludes with a direct comparison and a brief evaluative comment on the effectiveness of each text.

</td><td></td></tr>
</table>

This is a good answer that makes a range of relevant comparative points about the two texts. It is necessarily selective in its coverage, given the fact that two unseen texts have to be read, understood and written about in less than 45 minutes. This candidate might have been more specific about the use of sentence types in the two texts, and more direct quotation might have been used, but that does not detract from the clear success of this response. It addresses all of the comparative points required in the bullet points of the question and remains focused throughout on the key issue of how the texts achieve their purposes.

The Anthology question (Question 2)

AQA Examiner's tip

Do not have a preconceived idea of which texts you want to use in the examination. You need to know *all* of the texts in the Anthology so that you can make the right choice of texts to suit the question that is asked.

If the text is not relevant do not use it!

◼ Question 2

Choosing the right texts

The second of the two compulsory questions in your Unit 1 examination presents a particular focus, aspect or theme that is relevant to texts in the Anthology. You are free to select whichever pair of texts you can best write about in response to the question. This choice is both an opportunity and a potential danger. You should know all 33 texts well and be able to make informed choices about which two texts will best allow you to produce relevant comparative answers. Students who do not know the Anthology well enough could choose unsuitable texts, which would make it impossible to achieve a good mark for Question 2.

For example, the first of the specimen questions on the Anthology (see the Specimen questions on page 77) refers to texts that reveal a strong sense of the personality and attitudes of the writer. A student who entered the examination room determined to respond to this question by writing about Text 15: 'Hygiene Improvement Regulations' and Text 27: 'Workhouse Diets' would struggle to find anything relevant to say because neither text provides any significant evidence of the personality and values of its author.

The key point is this: you *must* know the 33 texts well, and you *must* make an informed choice about which pair of texts to write about *after* you have studied the question on the examination paper.

Timings

Question 1 is worth 32 marks and Question 2 is worth 64 marks. It is advisable to spend about 40 minutes on Question 1, which will leave you 65 minutes for Question 2.

It should be possible to decide fairly quickly which texts would be suitable choices and you will need to remind yourself of the details of the content, language and structure of the two texts you decide on.

Planning

Planning is as important as it is for Question 1 and you should aim to use the total time available in stages:

5 minutes	• Study the question and make certain that you understand what the task requires of you. • Consider which texts in the Anthology are most appropriate to the task and choose the two that you think will enable you to work to your best possible standard.
5–8 minutes	• Re-read the two texts, making notes on the significant features that are most relevant to the task. • Remember the point/example/comment technique as you work on the texts.
4–6 minutes	• Decide on a manageable number of key points (typically 5–7) that you intend to make in your answer, and this will help to determine the paragraph structure.
40-45 minutes	• Write the answer according to your plan, and keep track of the time. • Do not allow yourself to write at such length on any one section that you distort the overall shape of your answer or are forced to omit points that you intended to write about.
5 minutes	• If there is time, proofread your answer and correct any slips of the pen or other avoidable errors. • If there is no time for this do not worry. If you have followed the advice on what to do in the first hour, your answer should be worthy of a good mark even without a final check.

The wording of Question 2

As with Question 1, Question 2 also follows a predictable pattern. It always consists of three sentences, as in the following example:

Question 2

Some texts in the Anthology reveal a strong sense of the personality and attitudes of the writer.

Compare **two** texts from the Anthology in which aspects of each writer's personality and attitudes are prominent.

In your answer, write about some of the following **where appropriate**:

▦ contexts of production and reception	▦ word choice
▦ form and structure	▦ grammar
▦ figurative language	▦ layout and presentation
▦ sound patterning.	

The third and final sentence that starts 'In your answer' is the standard wording that will not change for the three-year life of the *Food Glorious Food* Anthology. It provides a clear reminder about what your answer should cover. The seven aspects referred to in this part of the question should be applied to the texts 'where appropriate', and these are important words. For example, it is possible that you will write about a text in which layout and presentation features play a vital part in the overall impact of the text. It is equally likely that another text you choose will contain no significant layout features. The first text would require some analysis of design features whereas it would be a waste of time to try to discuss design features in your second text.

The seven aspects common to all questions are:

▦ contexts of production and reception

▦ word choice

▦ form and structure

▦ grammar

▦ figurative language

▦ layout and presentation

▦ sound patterning.

It is part of the planning task to consider which of the seven aspects are most significant in your comparison of your two chosen texts. You might decide, for example, that four aspects are the most fruitful areas to concentrate on, and that you need to make brief comments on only one other aspect. In the limited time available you cannot possibly produce a detailed coverage of all seven areas, so it is far better to produce insightful comments on the key aspects than to spread your time thinly over all seven, some of which are less significant in your chosen texts.

In the Specimen questions opposite, Questions A to F illustrate various ways in which the principal examiner might set up Question 2 tasks. Studying these examples will:

▦ help you to become familiar with the style of questioning

▦ provide a bank of practice questions that you can tackle during the course

▦ provide a model for you to create your own examination-style questions (either working on your own or as part of a small group).

Practical activity

Analysing and understanding the questions

1 Analyse the wording of one of questions B to F, making a note of the key words in the first and second sentences of each question.

Notice that some of the key words appear both in the first sentence and in the second sentence. This repetition emphasises the importance of those key words to the specific task and is intended to help candidates to remain focused in their answers. Notice too that virtually every word in the second sentence is a key word that needs to be acted upon. This second sentence is the core of the question.

2 Now repeat this approach with the other remaining questions, noticing how key words from the first sentence are repeated in the second sentence.

Specimen questions for Question 2

A Some texts in the Anthology reveal a strong sense of the personality and attitudes of the writer.

Compare **two** texts from the Anthology in which aspects of each writer's personality and attitudes are prominent.

In your answer, write about some of the following **where appropriate**:

- contexts of production and reception
- word choice
- form and structure
- grammar
- figurative language
- layout and presentation
- sound patterning.

B People make choices about the food they eat and where they eat it.

Compare **two** texts from the Anthology which concern people's decisions about food.

In your answer, write about some of the following **where appropriate**:

- contexts of production and reception
- word choice
- form and structure
- grammar
- figurative language
- layout and presentation
- sound patterning.

C Some texts in the Anthology are mainly informative in their purpose.

Compare **two** texts in the Anthology which provide information as their main purpose.

In your answer, write about some of the following **where appropriate**:

- contexts of production and reception
- word choice
- form and structure
- grammar
- figurative language
- layout and presentation
- sound patterning.

Practical activity

1 For each of Questions A–F, select between three and five texts that would be suitable texts to write about if you were tackling the questions in the examination.

For each text write a brief explanation of why it would be a suitable choice. Be specific in explaining how the text is relevant to the question.

2 Of those texts, select the two you would actually write about if you were tackling the question in the examination and explain why you think a pairing of those two texts would offer good opportunities for comparison.

Practical activity

Now devise other questions on the Anthology, using Questions A–F as models for the wording and structure.

D The literary forms of poetry, drama and prose fiction are all represented in the Anthology.

Compare a pair of texts drawn from any **two** of these three literary genres.

In your answer, write about some of the following **where appropriate**:

- contexts of production and reception
- form and structure
- figurative language
- sound patterning.
- word choice
- grammar
- layout and presentation

E Some texts in the Anthology are intended not for a broad general audience of listeners and/or readers but for more specific groups.

Compare **two** texts from the Anthology which seem to have a restricted target audience.

In your answer, write about some of the following **where appropriate**:

- contexts of production and reception
- form and structure
- figurative language
- sound patterning.
- word choice
- grammar
- layout and presentation

F Some texts in the Anthology might cause readers to feel discomfort or even a sense of shock.

Compare **two** texts from the Anthology which might arouse these feelings in some readers.

In your answer, write about some of the following **where appropriate**:

- contexts of production and reception
- form and structure
- figurative language
- sound patterning.
- word choice
- grammar
- layout and presentation

Sample answer for Question 2

Sample answer to B

Text 25 is a 1920s advertisement for the breakfast cereal Grape Nuts and Text 22 is from the opening of Swift's satirical essay 'A Modest Proposal'. On one level both texts are based on the fact that we all make decisions about what we eat and, taken at face value, each text offers guidance about food choices. However, neither text can be fully understood if we simply take it literally. Text 25 clearly has a commercial purpose – to persuade consumers to buy Grape Nuts. Text 22 has as its ostensible purpose the presentation of the case for practising infant cannibalism as a solution to food shortages in Ireland in the early 18th century. Its true purpose, however, is to expose the horrors of exploitation of Irish peasants by English landlords. Swift's apparently amoral argument in favour of using human babies as food for the wealthy shocks us into thinking about the social and economic context that created extremes of poverty and wealth.

Text 25 consists of a hand-drawn sketch of a young woman beating her male opponent in a punting race, with the caption 'That surprising

Craig girl!' The text beneath this is in two main columns with a separate small information box. The appearance of the advertisement is dated, without the visual impact that we are used to in 21st-century advertising texts.

Text 22 has been reset in a modern font and consists of nine paragraphs of varying length. It has no significant layout features, although the language used is distinctive in a number of ways, especially in the use of low-key declarative sentences to express shockingly inhumane ideas. The text opens with a disarming reference to the 'number of souls in this Kingdom'. 'Souls' instead of 'people' almost lulls us into believing that we are about to read a religious treatise, but we are brought up short with the mention of wives as 'breeders', which suggests that these women are akin to farm animals whose only value is commercial. The main part of the opening paragraph is given over to the calculation of the likely numbers of children born to poor parents annually and their negligible monetary value up to the age of six. There is a complete lack of humanity in these calculations and Swift's reference to their picking up 'a livelihood by stealing' is not accompanied by any sense of moral disapproval.

Likewise, Swift's calculation that a boy or girl before the age of 12 is 'no saleable commodity' is completely devoid of human feeling, as is the comment that a 12-year-old will have cost at least four times as much in 'nutriment and rags' as he can be sold for. Swift has set us up for the next step in his argument – that an infant will fetch a high price if he is sold for food at a year old. The rest of the extract continues to treat human infants as if they are merely an alternative to a suckling pig or any other young farm animal reared for meat.

In contrast, Text 22 begins by stressing the individual accomplishments of Pam Craig. The opening sentence uses ellipsis to convey the idea that we are about to read the latest in a long line of her achievements: 'Pam Craig's latest is winning the half-mile punting singles.' The omission of a noun like 'feat' after 'latest' prepares us for the next sentence that tells us 'Pam could always be relied upon to do *something* unexpected'. This is a complete contrast to the dehumanised way in which Swift refers to people in Text 25. The second paragraph builds up the excitement of the race by describing how Pam overtook Tom McBride with 'a thrust that was as strong as it was graceful'. This contrasts with Tom 'splashing' and 'looking troubled'. '"The surprising Craig girl again!" said everyone' is the cue for the text to move on to its persuasive task. The next paragraph opens with the elliptical interrogative minor sentence 'Surprising?' and this combination of lexical and structural cohesion leads into a discussion of what it is that enables Pam to succeed. Pam herself gives the answer by means of direct speech: 'proper food – that especially'. This is confirmed by the editorial comment 'And she's right', followed by a repetition of 'proper food' and an explanation of why Grape Nuts provides the necessary nutrients so effectively. The structure of the text can be summarised as: 1 establishing the situation of Pam's success; 2 explaining the general basis for that success; 3 explaining the specific condition for that success (Grape Nuts).

Whereas the Grape Nuts text is delivered by an omniscient narrator, Swift's text is a first-person account in which he deliberately avoids explicitly persuasive language. His voice is at times self-effacing ('I … humbly propose my own thoughts'), which makes his suggestions the more shocking. He speaks of infant's flesh as being 'in season throughout the year', sees the consumption of Roman Catholic infants in Ireland as having the additional benefit of 'lessening the number of Papists among us' and even suggests that skin might be removed from the infants' carcasses to make 'admirable gloves for ladies, and summer boots for fine gentlemen'. The matter-of-fact tone is used to bypass moral judgements; Swift writes as if there is no moral distinction between the rich raising animals for food and using 'the carcass of a good fat child' merely as another source of animal protein. Swift also refers to the opinions of others who might be regarded as authorities – 'a very knowing American of my acquaintance', 'a principal gentleman of the County of Cavan' and 'our merchants' – to support his arguments.

By offering a 'solution' to the problem of unproductive peasants' children, Swift writes as if he is genuinely offering advice on food choices for wealthy landowners. His real purpose, though, is to attribute to the landlord class the moral responsibility for the poverty afflicting the peasant classes. Swift's true feelings rise to the surface in this sentence: 'I grant that this food will be somewhat dear, and therefore very proper for landlords, who, as they have already devoured most of the parents seem to have the best title to the children'.

In their different ways Texts 22 and 25 use the issue of food choices to serve particular purposes. The discourse style of Text 25 contrasts strongly with contemporary consumer advertising for food products, but the text and design seem well targeted at the readers of the magazine in which it first appeared. The Swift text achieves a powerful satirical effect but whether it penetrated the defences – or the moral vacancy – of its targets is perhaps doubtful. For some, the horror of Swift's suggestions might have provided an excuse to attack the writer rather than consider the underlying points he was trying to make. However, no modern reader could believe that Swift was really advocating cannibalism.

Commentary

This is a longer response than most candidates would be able to produce in the examination, but it does demonstrate a range of the possible analytical and comparative points that can be made about the chosen texts.

Although the advertisement clearly tries to influence consumers' food choices by promoting the benefits of Grape Nuts, the purpose of Swift's text is more complicated. It pretends to advocate eating the infants born to the Irish poor, but the candidate understands that it is actually a satirical attack on the landlords' exploitation of the poor. The candidate's opening paragraph justifies their choice of Text 22 as a valid one.

The answer makes some reference to all of the bullet point headings in the question except for 'sound patterning', which has limited relevance to these texts. The candidate's emphasis on the meanings and effects of the two texts allows reference to be made to grammar, word choice, text structure and so on throughout the answer and this served their purpose much more effectively than working sequentially through the bullet points, dealing with each one in turn. It is worth analysing this answer carefully, noting the way in which the paragraphs are linked and remain focused on the question, as well as the use of textual evidence in support of the points made.

A useful exercise would be to edit the answer to about 700 words to reflect what would be manageable within the examination time available. What would you take out and what would you leave in?

Glossary

A

Adjacency pair: an utterance by one speaker is followed by a reply from another, making an 'adjacent pair'. The first utterance could be a question or a greeting, and its content points to the kind of reply expected from the second person. So 'What time is it?' might be followed by 'It's 6pm'.

Agenda setting: the 'setting' or choice of a topic for a conversation or interaction.

Alliteration: the repetition of initial sounds such as in 'Full fathom five thy father lies'.

Ambiguity: the possibility of interpreting written or spoken words in more than one way. Sometimes words are used in an unintentionally ambiguous way, but creative or humorous language can use ambiguity deliberately to achieve particular effects.

Analogy: another word for comparison.

Antithesis: when opposing ideas or images are used for effect, for example: 'Man proposes; God disposes'.

Antonym: word that has the opposite meaning to another, such as alive/dead.

B

Bathos: a change in mood, usually from the serious to the more mundane or trivial.

Blank verse: unrhymed verse that follows a regular metrical pattern – usually 10 syllables to a line, with alternate stressed and unstressed syllables.

C

Cadence: another word for rhythm.

Caesurae: pauses within lines of verse (singular: caesura).

Collocation: the tendency of writers and speakers to place particular words in proximity with each other, such as 'Happy Father's Day' or 'Merry Christmas' (but not 'Merry Father's Day'). Collocations are often highly context dependent.

Colloquial: informal language of the kind used in everyday speech.

Complex: a complex sentence includes one or more subordinate clauses; e.g., 'I bought a new bicycle, *which was very expensive*, and I cycled home'.

Compound: a compound sentence contains more than one clause linked with a connective word such as 'but' and 'and'; e.g., 'I bought a new bicycle *and* I cycled home'.

Connotative: the emotional, individual and expressive meanings of a word or expression; these may not be exactly the same from one person to another.

Context dependent: word choice that varies depending upon the situation. For example, you will speak differently when asking for directions from a stranger compared with asking a close friend for a favour.

Context of production: the circumstances surrounding the writing or production of the text. These can include the personal situation of the author as well as aspects of the time in which they are writing (social conditions).

D

Declarative clause: a declarative clause is a statement that forms a section of a sentence, e.g. 'the pig is squealing'. (A clause contains at least a subject and verb, as shown here.)

Deixis: the use of expressions, typically in conversations, which refer to people, objects or ideas without explicitly naming or identifying them because the participants have shared knowledge. For example: 'I will buy the shoes at that shop over there' (the shop is not named).

Demotic: everyday, prosaic (ordinary) language.

Denotative: the literal or core meanings of a word or an expression.

Diatribe: a bitter condemnatory written or spoken attack, denouncing an idea or person.

Discourse marker: word or phrase that marks the boundary between topics.

Dramatic irony: this occurs when characters on stage are unaware of circumstances that the audience are well aware of.

Dynamic verb: verb that refers to a movement or action, such as run, leap, grasp.

E

Elegy: a meditative poem of lament, often commemorating someone's death, e.g. Gray's 'Elegy Written in a Country Churchyard'.

Elision: when sounds are omitted from words or phrases, such as 'don't' instead of 'do not'.

Ellipsis: the omission of an element of sentence structure: adjective 'elliptical'.

Enjambement: the technique of making the sense of a poem continue from one line to the next, creating a feeling of fluidity.

Etymology: the study of the origins and historical development of word meaning and usage.

Evaluative: an utterance that reveals attitudes and opinions. For example, 'I hate Marmite because it is too salty.' (Note that utterances can have more than one characteristic as this one is also expressive in its use of the verb 'hate'.)

Exclamative: phrase or sentence that is an exclamation, e.g. 'What a mess!' or 'Never!'

Expressive: a way of describing an utterance that reveals feelings, such as 'Oh, wonderful!'

F

Figurative language: this extends and alters the literal meaning of words. We might speak of someone having a 'sunny nature'. There is an implied comparison between their attitude and the brightness of the sun, but we do not assume the person has the qualities of the sun itself. The purpose of using figurative language in real talk or in fiction is to enable us to perceive something more vividly or allow us greater insight into a character or story.

Foregrounding: placing a particular word or phrase within a sentence so as to give it special prominence.

Free verse: a poem that is not constrained by regular metrical patterns, but is shaped by the speaking voice and the points being made.

G

Graphology: the study of writing systems, including the use of fonts of different styles and sizes.

H

Haiku: a word of Japanese origin that means a poem of three lines and a total of 17 syllables (line 1: five syllables, line 2: seven syllables, line 3: five syllables), e.g. William Carlos Williams' 'The Red Wheelbarrow'.

Hyperbole: exaggeration for effect, such as 'This pudding is sublime'.

I

Iambic: an iambic foot consists of an unstressed syllable followed by a stressed syllable, shown as u and / respectively. Five iambic feet make up a regular line, which has 10 syllables.

Idiom: expression that is often informal and figurative and is regularly used by a distinct group of people (such as English speakers in England), which outsiders might have difficulty interpreting at first. For example 'spill the beans' or 'the sky's the limit'.

Imagery: figurative language used to bring a scene, idea or object to life. It usually involves a comparison between two objects or ideas, such as 'The sun is like a red balloon'.

Imperative: an utterance that has the power of an order, such as 'Write that essay now'.

Intonation: the way in which the rising, falling and level tones of voice create sound patterns in phrases and sentences.

Irony: when a writer deliberately says one thing and means something else. For example, 'He was a very generous man and in his will he left his only sister his least-valuable stamp collection'. From this we can infer that he was the opposite of generous.

J

Juxtaposition: the placing together (or in close proximity) of visual or textual elements in order to draw out comparisons or contrasts.

L

Linear narrative: a storyline where events clearly follow in chronological sequence.

M

Metre: from the Greek word 'metron', which means measure. The measurement of a line of poetry, including its length and its number of stresses.

Minor sentence: a sentence that contains no main verb, e.g. 'Ready?'; 'So what?'; 'Nonsense!'; 'Two seniors please.' Minor sentences are heavily context dependent; i.e. they are intelligible only in the time and place in which they occur.

Monosyllabic lexis: words made up of one syllable, e.g. cat, house, tune.

Motif: a dominant theme or a recurring symbol.

N

Narrative: an account where events related (in speech or writing) are connected.

Narrative sequence: the order in which a story is told.

O

Omniscient narrator: the storyteller (the author) has a complete knowledge of all characters and all situations. The story is presented using the third person (he/she/it) rather than the first person method (I).

Onomatopoeia: words that sound like their meaning. For example 'slush', 'snap' or 'crisp'.

Oxymoron: an expression that seems contradictory, e.g. 'living death'.

P

Paralinguistic feature: sound that is used in addition to or alongside the language system, e.g. grunt, cough, laugh, and aspects of voice quality such as intonation, pitch, loudness and speed.

Parallelism: when similar grammatical constructions are used and placed next to each other (in parallel). For example 'a sharpening wind, a blackening sky'.

Pastiche: an imitation of the style of a text.

Pentameter: (from the Latin for 'five') refers to the number of metrical feet in the line.

Personification: a type of figurative language when a writer treats an inanimate object or idea as if it were human. For example, 'The wind sighed'.

Phatic talk: social talk that helps to facilitate interactions, e.g. 'How are you?'

Polysyllabic lexis: words made up of more than one syllable, such as 'chocolate' or 'catastrophe'.

Premodifier: in a noun phrase such as 'a nasty knock on the nose', the premodifier is the word or phrase that precedes the noun 'knock'. Post-modifiers occur after the phrase. So 'nasty' is a premodifier that tells us more about the noun, and 'on the nose' is a post-modifier that gives us additional information.

R

Register: variety of language that is used for particular purposes or within a particular social context.

Repairs and reformulations: when a speaker makes corrections to their own speech. For example, a speaker says: 'He, no she, walked into the room, or rather staggered slowly.' The speaker repairs (corrects) and changes the pronoun from he to she and then reformulates by altering the verb and qualifying it.

Revenge tragedy: a play where one or more characters are spurred on by the desire to avenge perceived wrongs that have been committed against them. Their vengeance usually involves much bloodshed.

Rhetorical question: question that expects no answer from the listener or reader. It is often used as part of a persuasive strategy.

Rhythm: the rhythm of a poem refers to the pulse or beat that the listener perceives.

S

Satirical: writing in a satirical way involves adopting a mocking tone, but with serious undertones. Dickens mocks (satirises) the treatment of workhouse inmates, with the serious intent of drawing the reader's attention to the problems.

Schema: a set of expectations in a given situation. For example, when attending a job interview there is a schema (an expected framework) that will influence what you do and say.

Semantics: the study of the system of meanings within a language.

Simple: a simple sentence contains at least one subject and one verb, for example, 'I cycled'. Or the sentence can have an object; e.g., 'I' (subject) 'bought' (verb) 'a new bicycle' (object).

Sonnet: a traditional poetic form that usually has 14 lines of 10 syllables each, and with a regular rhyming and stress pattern, e.g. Shakespeare's sonnets.

Stanza: group of lines that forms a unit in a poem (often called a verse).

Stress: emphasis on a syllable or particular word.

Stressed syllable: a unit of pronunciation that is emphasised (this is shown as an oblique stroke, '/').

Style: in written texts this is the choice and arrangement of words that create a particular effect. Jonathan Swift spoke of 'proper words in proper places'.

Subordinate clause: a clause (which usually contains a subject, verb and object) that gives additional information to the main clause, and is subordinate to it. For example, 'I bought a new bicycle (main clause), which was very expensive (subordinate adjectival clause, describing the bicycle)'.

Syllable: unit of pronunciation where there is one vowel sound. Monosyllabic words have one syllable: 'I', 'cat', 'me'. Polysyllabic words have several syllables:

u /   /   u   / u /
re-venge, wel-come, en-ter-tain.

Synonym: word that has the same or very similar meaning to another, such as bucket/pail.

Syntax: the way in which words are arranged to show the meaning. The word originates from the Greek word for arrangement: 'syntaxis'.

T

Tag question: a question usually added to a declarative statement to make it interrogative.

Transactional talk: language that is used in 'transactions', such as when you are buying chocolate or arranging for a car service.

Typography: the style and appearance of the print. This includes the kind of font chosen and its size and arrangement on the page.

U

Unstressed syllable: a unit of pronunciation that is not emphasised (this is shown as 'u').

Index

Key terms are in **bold**.